The Body "Knows" COOKBOOK

The Body "Knows" COOKBOOK

By CAROLINE SUTHERLAND

Companion to
The Body "Knows" series

BALBOA
PRESS
A DIVISION OF HAY HOUSE

Sutherland Communications, Inc.
1 Lake Louise Drive, #34
Bellingham, WA 98229

Visit online at: www.carolinesutherland.com

Book design by: Christian Kelly
Photo of the author by: Erin Fiedler

ISBN: 978-1-4525-0065-2 (sc)
ISBN: 978-1-4525-0121-5 (e)

Balboa Press books may be ordered through booksellers or by contacting:

Balboa Press
A Division of Hay House
1663 Liberty Drive
Bloomington, IN 47403
www.balboapress.com
1-(877) 407-4847

Because of the dynamic nature of the Internet, any Web addresses or links contained in
this book may have changed since publication and may no longer be valid. The views
expressed in this work are solely those of the author and do not necessarily reflect the
views of the publisher, and the publisher hereby disclaims any responsibility for them.

The author of this book does not dispense medical advice or prescribe the use of
any technique as a form of treatment for physical, emotional, or medical problems
without the advice of a physician, either directly or indirectly. The intent of the
author is only to offer information of a general nature to help you in your quest for
emotional and spiritual well-being. In the event you use any of the information
in this book for yourself, which is your constitutional right, the author, Sutherland
Communications, Inc., realetd parties, and the publisher assume no responsibility
for your actions, with respect to loss, damage, or injury caused or alleged to be
caused directly or indirectly by the information contained in this book..

Printed in the United States of America

Balboa Press rev. date: 10/28/2010

Dedication

This book is dedicated to my mother, who taught me how to cook, and to all my friends and clients who have discovered for themselves that they feel so much better when they understand that "The Body Knows"—what it wants them to eat!

CONTENTS

INTRODUCTION

"I will always be grateful to Caroline Sutherland for her guidance and refinement of my food choices. In order to stay very healthy and have lots of energy, I no longer eat wheat, dairy, sugar, corn, soy, citrus, beans, or caffeine. I am very blessed to be able to grow my own food.

"My main diet consists of protein and vegetables with some fruit. I am not a vegetarian; however, I do eat lots of vegetables. I eat fish and organic meats and fowl. Animal protein is very good for my body. I use coconut oil, butter, or duck fat for cooking; and flaxseed oil or olive oil for salads."

— Louise L. Hay

The Body "Knows" Cookbook is designed to be a companion to *The Body "Knows": How to Tune In to Your Body and Improve Your Health.* So in order to get the most from this cookbook, do be sure to read that original book.

Given nearly three decades of clinical experience, there is absolutely no question in my mind that no matter what a person's state of health, the fuel/food that the body is fed will affect his or her cell tissue—immediately. For anyone to suggest otherwise is missing the key part of the health equation.

Most of the recipes in *The Body "Knows" Cookbook* are gleaned from many years of working with people with food

1

allergies, my own favorites, and the terrific help of my niece Georgia Morley.

Georgia has an extensive background in food and catering for the movie industry. She feeds the "stars" and is a highly inventive cook. Where I tend to cook on the basic side, Georgia is a master at blending interesting textures, exotic food items, and flavors. At any of our family gatherings, we're a happy bunch when Georgia is in the kitchen.

Here are a few words from Georgia herself:

> *Ever since I was a small child, I suffered from food sensitivity without knowing it. As I grew older, the symptoms became more challenging to my health and well-being. With encouragement from my aunt Caroline Sutherland, I omitted dairy products and sugar from my diet altogether. I began to reap the rewards immediately. My headaches, sore throats, lethargy, and small hives ceased – and I lost weight. I just generally felt 100 percent better. After having my first child, I noticed that he too suffered from skin irritation, dark eye circles, irritability, and lethargy. We removed all dairy products completely, and he has thrived. He loves goat milk, rice milk, and other dairy alternatives. And now he can occasionally enjoy a small amount of cow's dairy without any consequence.*
>
> *As a chef, I'm extremely excited to be a part of a book such as this. I've become a true believer in the role that food sensitivity plays in our lives and the importance of cooking taste bud–pleasing meals that avoid the*  *foods to which so many people are sensitive. I hope you enjoy this book and the journey to happy, healthy eating.*

If you are battling food allergies or the Candida yeast syndrome, you are not alone. Many years ago, the discovery of **multiple food sensitivities plus** an overgrowth of Candida albicans yeast called for a major overhaul of my eating habits.

At that time, I was a busy career woman and wife, as well as the mother of two daughters. However, the choice was obvious: for over 20 years, I had suffered from cyclical bouts of depression, fatigue, respiratory problems, arthritic symptoms, and the early warning signs of multiple sclerosis.

At first, I felt justly deprived of my favorite foods. But by cleaning up my diet and watching what I ate, my symptoms began to improve in a matter of weeks. Eventually, they disappeared completely.

My aim in the book is to introduce *you* to tasty foods that will help to control the overgrowth of Candida albicans yeast, and ones that won't trigger histamine reactions and the consequent weight gain and related symptoms.

If you have thought that the path to vibrant health is a complete mystery, and you have not considered food allergies/sensitivities as part of the equation, I hope that *The Body "Knows" Cookbook* will open a new and exciting door for you.

———————

The plan when using this cookbook is to remember that the body "knows" what it needs in terms of fuel/food. When we give the body what it wants, miraculously, an improvement in health occurs. This is not the time to go out on a limb in the "weird" food department. While you are getting used to a program, keep things simple. Please don't add stress to your already busy life.

I have broken the book down into simple sections. Lunch and dinner menus are interchangeable, as are salads and soups. I have indicated where people who have digestive problems need to take caution with certain spices and ingredients. I have also added a useful section for children.

Carbohydrate grams are kept low unless otherwise specified. You will probably notice that when you put carbohydrates into your system, especially at breakfast and lunch, you will probably have low energy, hunger pangs, and cravings for more carbs. Low-carbohydrate vegetables, on the other hand, will not initiate this response.

Remember, the most common food sensitivities are: dairy products, wheat/flour, corn, soy, and yeast. It goes without saying that sugar and caffeine are obvious culprits.

Take "food families" into consideration as well. Coconuts and dates are related. Chocolate and cola are related. Watermelon and cucumber are related to zucchini. If potatoes give you hives or tomatoes give you arthritis, you need to know that these belong to the same "nightshade" food family (and so do peppers). For a complete list of food families, refer to the section in the back of this book.

Do your best to "rotate" foods; that is, don't consume the same foods day after day after day. Usually the foods you consume the most, or are addicted to, are the ones to which you are allergic or sensitive. Rotate your foods, sampling as many different items as you can.

I find that it really helps to have food on hand. No one wants to come home to an empty refrigerator and nothing healthy to eat. Plan ahead and follow the "three-meal rule." That means knowing where your next three meals are located. Think of the meal you are eating and plan for the following two meals. This offers a sense of reassurance that you will be able to eat "on program" and not be scrambling to find something to eat.

When it comes to changing eating patterns, attitude is all-important. Think positively! So the rest of the world is eating nachos—treat yourself to smoked salmon or cashews! You'll soon find out that there are plenty of alternatives out there just waiting to be tried.

Things to think about before getting started:

- Buy whole, fresh, organic foods where possible.
- Take the time to read labels and locate hidden food culprits.
- Drink six to eight glasses of purified or spring water per day.
- If you are not trying to lose weight, add carbohydrates (starch) to every meal.
- If you are pregnant or lactating, consult your doctor before starting any program.
- If you are looking for energy and mental clarity, keep your carbohydrates low.

(**A note about soy**: It is becoming more apparent that soy is *not* the so-called miracle food. Soy is one of the "big five" food sensitivities because it is hard to digest, it can suppress thyroid function, and it affects the way your body absorbs iron and B vitamins. Germany, the United Kingdom, and Israel have banned the sale of soy infant formulas because of soy's estrogenic effects. Do keep in mind that soy sauce, miso, and tempeh are fermented products, so they should have no deleterious effects if used sparingly. For more information about soy, read: *The Whole Soy Story* by Kaayla Daniel, Ph.D., or visit: **www.thewholesoystory.com**.)

Congratulations on taking those first steps to broadening your food horizons—your body truly "knows." Create and strengthen new habits and anticipate the benefits you will feel. In a few short weeks of avoiding your "offending foods," you will be able to return to having the occasional "no-no" without too many ill effects. In the meantime, remember what the ancient Greek physician Hippocrates said: "Let food be thy medicine and medicine be thy food"!

BREAKFAST

I do not eat fruit with my breakfast. I occasionally have fruit during the day or after dinner, several hours after a meal. I feel better and have more energy, mental clarity, and stamina—and no food cravings—if I stay away from carbohydrates at breakfast and lunch.

If you like toast, try 100% rye bread, millet bread, rice bread, or any other alternative breads that are available at any health-food store. Look for almond-flour muffins in the dessert section. Avoid spelt and kamut, which are ancient, non-hybridized strains of wheat that, over time, may cause food reactions. Try some of the unusual breads and cracker recipes in this book. Jam has too many carbohydrates, though—save it for the occasional treat.

Here are a few breakfast alternatives:

- Organic turkey sausages or chicken sausages; or salmon, poultry, or meat from the previous night's dinner, with or without steamed vegetables. If you are not allergic/sensitive to beans, try a bean-and-vegetable scramble.

- Breakfast on-the-run might be 2 Wasa (whole rye) crackers with almond butter.

- Try Louise Hay's favorite breakfast: sautéed grated zucchini in coconut oil with sautéed wild salmon or tilapia.

The rest of the chapter features some other excellent choices for your morning meal.

EGGS

Eggs make a great breakfast, especially omelet-style with chopped, steamed vegetables—such as cauliflower, broccoli, zucchini, ½ a carrot for color, green beans, etc. Cook and drain the vegetables first, before adding the beaten eggs. Add olive oil, coconut oil, salt and pepper, spices, or herbs as desired. I like a herbal blend called "Spike," which is available at health-food stores.

Eggs can be an allergen for some people. This sensitivity can manifest as nausea, headaches, digestive problems, rashes, or mood changes. Eggs can often be difficult for an overloaded liver to handle. See your local practitioner for advice on liver cleansing.

Scrambles

2 whole eggs or 3 egg whites, whisked gently with a fork.

Choose any of the following ingredients to add to your scramble:

- 1 green onion, chopped
- 1 clove garlic (note that many people are sensitive to garlic), minced
- ½ red, green, or yellow bell pepper
- ½ cup broccoli or zucchini, chopped
- 1 cup fresh spinach
- 1 tomato (may be too acidic for certain digestive systems), chopped

Choose one of the following ingredients to add to your scramble:

- ½ cup smoked salmon, chopped
- ½ cup cooked chicken
- 1 spicy sausage, cooked and sliced

- 2 slices crispy bacon, crumbled
- ½ cup cooked beans

In a medium skillet, heat 1 tsp butter, olive oil, or cold-pressed vegetable oil. Add chosen ingredients and sauté until soft or heated. Add whisked eggs or egg whites and cook until medium firm. Season with salt and pepper

Note: For a zippy flavor, add hot sauce; diced jalapeño peppers; a sprinkle of dried basil, thyme, or oregano; or some chopped fresh herbs such as dill, parsley, or basil. But remember, if you have a sensitive digestive system, stay away from hot, spicy foods and raw garlic and onions.

Traveling tip: Order eggs with bacon or smoked salmon. Omelets work well. Carry your own bread or Wasa crackers or order ½ cup hash browns. No toast—any variety of restaurant "toast" contains wheat.

Baked Dijon and Tomato Eggs

1 or 2 eggs, per person
1 tsp mayonnaise per egg
1 tsp Dijon mustard per egg
1 large tomato, sliced
Salt and pepper, to taste

Preheat oven to 350° F.

Lightly grease a muffin tin with vegetable oil. Place a tomato slice in the bottom of each cup, and crack an egg on top. Mix mayonnaise and Dijon mustard; spoon 1 tsp of mixture on top of the egg. Place in oven on the top rack and cook until slightly browned and eggs are cooked.

Bake approximately 5–10 minutes for soft, 10–12 minutes for medium, and 15 minutes for well-done eggs.

Note: The tomato can be replaced with smoked salmon or smoked turkey.

PANCAKES

If you are looking for a variation on the bread theme, try making pancakes. Use a hot, greased pan—cast iron works well. Wait until bubbles form and the pancake edges are dry and start to pull up from the pan before you attempt to flip them.
Combinations:

- Millet: 2 parts millet flour to 1 part tapioca or arrowroot flour plus water.
- Rice: 4 parts rice flour to 1 part tapioca or arrowroot flour plus water.
- Oat or barley: just add water to oat or barley flour (avoid if wheat sensitive, for the first 30 days).

The above batters should be very thin and turn lacy when the batter hits the hot pan. The result will be a thin crepe.

- Buckwheat: 1 cup buckwheat flour, 1 tsp baking soda, and water to create a thick batter; add an egg, mashed banana, or blueberries. Makes a thick griddlecake.

- Chickpea: 1 cup of this garbanzo-bean flour (chana or besan flour as it is called in East Indian markets), 1 tsp baking soda, and water to create a thick batter. This has a slight legume favor but makes an excellent sandwich base for lunch with mayo, sprouts, avocado, tomato, tuna, etc.

Note: None of these pancakes is low in carbohydrates.

Be very careful that making "unusual" and alternative grain pancakes does not add to your stress level. Remember that bread alternatives and delicious wheat-free crackers abound in health-food stores, along with tapioca and arrowroot flours.

Apple-Cinnamon Pancakes

2 cups chickpea flour
1 tsp baking powder
1 tsp cinnamon
1 tsp grated nutmeg
½ tsp salt
½ cup rice milk or water
3 eggs (separated)
1 cup apples, peeled and chopped
1 tsp grated lemon rind
Coconut oil or butter

Combine all dry ingredients. In another bowl, combine all wet ingredients except for the egg whites. Whisk egg whites until light and fluffy; set aside. Stir the liquid into dry ingredients. Allow mixture to sit covered for 20 minutes; fold in egg whites at the last minute. Heat the griddle or frying pan to medium-high heat. Add oil or butter and wait until pan is hot. See notes at the beginning of the pancake section before flipping.

Serve hot with a little stevia and a sprinkling of cinnamon.

Note: Stevia is a natural sweetener available in powder or liquid form at health-food stores, and it is *very* sweet. Also, this recipe is not low in carbohydrates.

Gluten-Free Flax, Blueberry, and Banana Pancakes

1 small (or ½ large) apple, roughly chopped

1 banana, mashed
1 large egg
3 Tbsp flaxseed meal
½ cup brown rice flour
½ tsp baking powder
1 Tbsp water
1 pinch kosher or sea salt
½ cup blueberries

Put the apple and banana in a food processor or blender and pulse a few times to chop it up. Add the rest of the ingredients except for the blueberries, and pulse gently.

Heat a small nonstick skillet over medium-high heat and spray lightly with nonstick cooking spray. Pour the batter into the hot pan and turn the heat down to low. Sprinkle the blueberries on top of the batter and gently press them into the top of the pancake.

Cook for about 6 minutes or until the edges look dry, the bottom is browned, and the pancake will slide around in the pan after it has been loosened with a spatula. Flip the pancake over and cook for another 4–5 minutes. The pancake should feel firm to the touch. Flip onto a plate (blueberry-side up) and serve.

Delicious Basic Pancake and Waffle Mix

½ cup spelt flour
1 cup tapioca flour
1 tsp cream of tartar
¼ tsp baking soda

This mixture can be doubled, tripled, and stored.

Mix together:

3 beaten eggs or egg replacer (health-food store item)

3 Tbsp vegetable oil
½ cup rice milk, almond milk, or alternative milk

Add wet ingredients to 1½ cups of dry mix above. Mix and add water to desired consistency. Place batter on hot griddle or hot waffle iron.

- For a hearty pancake or waffle, add ½ cup cooked millet or assorted cooked grain to the batter.

- Breakfast variation: sprinkle pancake with toasted cashews, blueberries, peach chunks, or banana slices.

- Lunch variation: plain pancake or waffle topped with sprouts, avocado, mayonnaise and smoked salmon, assorted meats or beans (hummus), etc.

Note: Cook quantities for later use; reheat in toaster or toaster oven. This recipe is high in carbohydrates.

HOT OATMEAL ALTERNATIVE

1 part whole quinoa, millet, or amaranth (rinsed)
2 parts water

Cook 15–20 minutes or until grain is cooked but not mushy.
Serve with a pat of butter, coconut oil, and alternative milk if desired, plus a generous sprinkle of roasted nuts.

Note: Of all these grains, quinoa (pronounced *keen-wah*) is my favorite.

LUNCH

When you're eating out, salad bars are an easy way to avoid offending foods. Choose the oil-and-vinegar dressing instead of "creamy" dairy-based dressings, and ask for a protein choice on the side. Carry Wasa or Kavli crackers or order rice or potatoes as a starch. If you are stuck in a fast-food restaurant, buy the burger, throw away the bun, and eat the fries.

You'll notice that the majority of this chapter centers on salads and soups. However,

people with sensitive or fragile digestive systems do not do well with salads—sautéed or steamed vegetables with the lunch meal are best.

I often save leftover vegetables from dinner and mix with an avocado and a creamy vinaigrette dressing for lunch. Or if I don't feel like chopping a bunch of vegetables, I make roll-ups by placing my protein selection in a large lettuce or cabbage leaf and rolling it up. Roll-ups can be made more exotic by adding any of the vegetables or ingredients from the "Loaded" Salad recipe below. Thinly sliced ham or turkey slices can also be used as a base for roll-ups.

Occasionally, I enjoy 2 buttered Wasa, Kavli, or Finn Crisp (whole rye) crackers with my lunch. But I usually stay away from carbohydrates with this meal also. I find that I have better energy this way.

SALADS

The "Loaded" Salad

This is a large salad composed of a variety of interesting lettuce plus chopped green vegetables of any sort. (Some people are sensitive to the cabbage or mustard food family—broccoli, cauliflower, cabbage, Brussels sprouts, kale, etc. These vegetables can cause digestive problems such as discomfort, gas, or burping.)

Add any of the following ingredients to your salad: red pepper (watch tomatoes—many people are sensitive to the acid in this fruit/vegetable); toasted sunflower seeds; chopped olives; avocado; marinated artichoke hearts; marinated cold vegetables from last night's dinner; cubed cold chicken or turkey; chunks of cold or canned salmon; tuna, beef, or lamb; or, if you're not allergic, beans (garbanzos are delicious).

Sprinkle the top of your salad with toasted pecan halves or toasted walnut pieces and, as an alternative to dairy products, goat feta cheese or sheep cheddar or sheep Romano cheese. Sheep and goat products are from different food families, not from a cow, therefore they do not usually trigger histamine reactions in dairy-sensitive people. Butter *is* a dairy product— but because it contains very few milk solids, which can trigger immune reactions, it is usually permissible.

Remember: Eggs are not dairy products.

Marinated Salad

4 cups lightly steamed vegetables, cold
1 whole avocado, sliced
⅓ cup creamy vinaigrette dressing
¼ cup toasted pecans—or any nut
Shrimp, cold salmon, poultry, or meat (optional)

Mix ingredients together and serve.

Shrimp and Spinach Salad

1 bunch spinach, washed and trimmed
½ lb. hand-peeled shrimp
Juice of 1 lemon or lime (may be omitted if sensitive to citrus)
1 tsp fresh grated lemon rind
2 Tbsp olive oil
2 Tbsp red wine vinegar (may be omitted)
2 Tbsp mayonnaise
1 tsp grainy mustard
2 tsp toasted sesame seeds

Wash and pat dry trimmed spinach.

In a small bowl, combine lemon or lime juice, lemon rind, olive oil, vinegar, mayonnaise, and grainy mustard.

Toss half of the dressing with spinach just before serving. Sprinkle shrimp over salad; add remaining dressing, and sprinkle with sesame seeds.

Roasted Beet Salad

8 raw beets, unpeeled and thinly sliced
2 Tbsp olive oil
Juice of 1 lemon (can be omitted if sensitive to citrus)

2 tsp red wine vinegar
½ cup dill, chopped
Sea salt and cracked black pepper, to taste

Preheat oven to 350° F.

Toss the sliced beets with olive oil so that they're well coated, and place on a baking sheet. Roast in oven until the beets look glossy and are soft (approximately ½ hour); remove and place in a bowl, allowing the beets to cool.

In a small bowl, combine lemon juice, red wine vinegar, fresh dill, salt, and pepper. Toss dressing with beets. Serve alone or atop a mixed green salad.

Note: Not low in carbohydrates: 1 cup beets = 12 carbohydrate grams.

Louise's Favorite Salad

1 cup of each:

- Finely grated beets
- Finely grated radish
- Finely grated zucchini
- The juice of 1 lemon
- ¼ cup olive or flaxseed oil

Eat as is or add to a bowl of greens.

Ukrainian Cucumber Salad

2 long English cucumbers, thinly sliced
Juice of 1 lemon (can be omitted if sensitive to citrus)
½ diced red onion (can be omitted if sensitive to onion)
1 tsp lemon rind, grated
2 tsp white wine vinegar

½ cup plain goat yogurt
1 tsp parsley, chopped
1 tsp paprika
Salt and pepper, to taste

Add all the ingredients together and toss until cucumbers are completely covered in dressing. Season with salt and pepper.

Note: Some people find cucumbers hard to digest.

Sesame Coleslaw (or Cabbage Salad)

Here's what Teresa said about this salad:

Your simple cabbage salad was the "hit" of our family picnic yesterday — seriously! After we ate dinner, some of the aunts started commenting on this delicious salad, and they began a table-by-table search of the person who brought it. Finally, our table was approached, and when they found out it was brought by me, they demanded to know the recipe. And this is from a family who is extremely traditional — meat, potatoes, gravy, and any dessert you can set out. Raw veggies? Salad? Don't bother! I've had many compliments on this salad before, so I took my chances when bringing it to this reunion. I'm so glad they enjoyed it, and I wanted you to know that the recipe that you shared continues to be shared! Many blessings, Teresa

½ head red or green cabbage, shredded or finely sliced
2 large carrots, peeled and grated
2 stalks celery, diced
1 medium apple, peeled and chopped
1 red bell pepper, diced (optional)
1 Tbsp mayonnaise
3 tsp tamari sauce
Juice of 1 orange (can be omitted if sensitive to citrus)

Juice of 1 lime (substitute 1 Tbsp vinegar for citrus juices)
⅓ cup toasted sesame seeds
¼ cup walnut pieces
1 Tbsp sesame or vegetable oil
Salt and pepper, to taste

Combine all ingredients, coating the cabbage entirely in the dressing, and chill for at least 20 minutes. Serve with Easy Corn Bread wedges (see Accompaniments chapter) and protein of choice.

Variation: Garnish with a sprinkling of fresh strawberries or raspberries.

Flavor variation: Add 1 Tbsp finely chopped fresh ginger to coleslaw mixture.

Scrumptious Mid-Summer Salad

1 head bib or butter lettuce, gently torn
1 medium avocado (whole), cubed
1 medium peach, peeled and chunked
¼ cup artichoke hearts, drained and chopped
¼ cup toasted pine nuts
¼ cup crumbled sheep milk Roquefort cheese (available at specialty cheese shops or Costco)
1 tbsp chopped fresh tarragon

Dressing:
⅓ cup olive oil
2 Tbsp white wine vinegar
Dash of salt

Combine dressing ingredients and shake in a small covered jar. Arrange lettuce pieces on plates. Decorate with avocado, artichoke hearts, pine nuts, peach chunks, and crumbled Roquefort. Drizzle dressing over salad and garnish with fresh tarragon. Serves 2.

Note: Be very sparing with any Roquefort or blue cheese due to mold content.

Louise Hay's Salad in a Blender

This blended salad is the perfect thing to have on a hot summer day, or anytime you are in a hurry.

Just combine the following in a blender and off you go! It's delicious and nutritious.

- 1 cup V-8 or tomato juice
- 1 tsp apple cider vinegar or lemon juice
- Diced vegetables, such as: carrots, zucchini, celery, romaine lettuce, any kind of sprouts, cucumbers, radishes, tomatoes, or bell peppers. Use any amount you wish.

You can add a bit of salad dressing to taste, and/or seaweed* flakes and sea salt. I like to add a raw egg yolk for protein.

Serve in an attractive tall glass.

* Seaweeds and dulse contain iodine, necessary for thyroid health.

Tomato, Onion, and Cumin-Seed Salad

4 large tomatoes, sliced
1 red onion, thinly sliced
2 Tbsp cumin seeds, toasted (heat in a small frying pan till golden)
2 Tbsp balsamic vinegar

1 Tbsp honey
Sea salt and cracked black pepper, to taste

Arrange tomatoes in a circular fan shape on a deep plate; arrange onion slices on top. In a small bowl, combine cumin seed, balsamic vinegar, and honey. Drizzle dressing over the salad and season with cracked pepper and sea salt.

Roasted Garlic Caesar

1 head romaine lettuce, washed and torn into bite-size pieces
1 egg yolk, whisked
2 anchovy fillets, chopped finely
3 garlic cloves, roasted in the oven (see below)
3 Tbsp olive oil
3 Tbsp white wine vinegar
¼ cup olive oil
Salt and pepper, to taste

Roasting garlic:
1 large head (cluster) of garlic
1 Tbsp olive oil

Cut away the first ½" from the top of the garlic cluster. Place garlic on foil and pour olive oil over the top. Seal garlic in the foil and place in the oven on a baking sheet for about 40 minutes. The aroma will give you the biggest hint that the garlic is done— it should be nicely brown and squeeze easily from its skin.

Add 3 roasted garlic cloves to the egg mixture. Slowly whisk olive oil from pan into egg mixture, adding white wine vinegar and additional oil until thick. Toss salad with dressing so that the lettuce is entirely coated. Add black pepper and sea salt to taste.

You may add ½ cup cooked shrimp, grilled chicken breast, cold roast beef, or roast lamb to each portion of this salad to make a full meal.

Note: The remaining roasted garlic may be sealed and stored in the refrigerator for up to 4 days. Also, cooked garlic is much easier to digest than raw garlic.

Thai Noodle Salad

1 pkg vermicelli rice noodles or rice pasta noodles
2 Tbsp fresh cilantro, chopped
1 red bell pepper, slivered
1 yellow bell pepper, slivered
1 cup romaine lettuce, chopped
1 cup broccoli florets, blanched
1 cup bean sprouts
1 Tbsp sesame or vegetable oil
2 Tbsp tamari sauce
2 Tbsp rice wine vinegar
1 Tbsp lime juice—optional
1 tsp chili flakes—optional
Dash of oyster sauce—optional
2 Tbsp toasted cashews, almonds, or sunflower seeds, chopped

Drop vermicelli noodles into 4 cups briskly boiling water. Cook for 4 or 5 minutes until soft. Drain noodles and cool under running cold water to prevent them from sticking together. Toss noodles with sesame oil; set aside.

In a medium-sized bowl, combine all vegetables. In a small bowl, combine tamari, lime juice, oyster sauce, and chili flakes. Toss the vegetables with dressing and place on top of the noodles. Garnish with toasted nuts and serve with chopsticks for fun eating.

Note: Add grilled chicken breast, ½ cup shrimp, or other protein choice to this salad. Not low in carbohydrates.

DRESSINGS

Use any oil-and-vinegar dressing. Even if you are focusing on controlling Candida yeast when fermented items should be avoided, vinegar in small amounts should be permissible. Sensitivity to ferment usually manifests in nasal congestion, a runny nose, postnasal drip, or headaches.

People who are not sensitive to citrus fruits (lemon, orange, and grapefruit) may use lemon or lime juice in place of vinegar in salad dressings. Some people go as far as straining raspberries and using the juice as a base for their dressing. It is not necessary to add this kind of stress to your life. For the first 30 days of your program, stay away from dressings containing sugar and dairy products. Read labels. Add mayonnaise to your dressing to make it creamy, if you desire—mayonnaise is made from eggs and oil, so it does not contain dairy products.

When I'm at home, I like to make my own dressing:

- 3 Tbsp flaxseed oil (high in essential fatty acids) or olive oil
- 2 tsp vinegar—apple cider, balsamic, raspberry, or rice wine variety
- ½ tsp creamy Dijon mustard

- Pinch of coarse, Celtic sea salt
- Fresh ground pepper

In place of Dijon mustard, I use fresh herbs such as chopped basil, dill, parsley, or my favorite—fresh tarragon.

As an alternative flavor, I use sesame seeds, fresh ginger, and 1 tsp soy sauce or ½ tsp wasabi paste.

To make the dressing creamy, add the olive oil very slowly to the vinegar and other ingredients and whisk or blend well.

Shake well in a glass jar and serve over salad.

SOUPS

Basic Beef Broth

Many people ask me for my soup recipes, especially my Basic Beef Broth.

When a body is sick or in a weakened state, nurturing soups, which are easy to digest, can provide a welcome change from solid food. Chicken soup and chicken broth are well-known healing elixirs, but many people overlook the benefits of naturally occurring iron, B vitamins, and nutritious marrow that are found in beef and beef bones. This beef broth in particular has been useful for many of my clients. The directions are so easy:

- Purchase a large bag of beef bones. Choose bones with some meat left on them. Beef ribs or rib bones would work nicely.

- Put the bones on a baking sheet or in a shallow roasting pan and bake at 325° F for about 2 hours. (The purpose of first baking the bones is to remove fat and to enhance the flavor of the brew.)

- Remove the bones from the oven and boil on a low simmer for another 2 hours. Strain and drink the broth.

As an added taste, add a quartered onion or a carrot to the roasting bones. These can be boiled in the pot with the bones.

Be sure you are aware of onion sensitivities before adding these to the mixture. Salt may be added to the broth if tolerated and desired.

Drink as much of the broth as you desire. When people are weak or very ill, I recommend approximately 4-6 cups per day. The broth may also be consumed as a beverage, along with regular meals.

Louise's Bone Broth

Here is another very simple recipe for broth.

In a large bag in the freezer, collect bones from chicken, duck, lamb, or beef—dinner scraps. Feel free to also add any vegetable scraps or peelings—such as skins of onions or garlic, trimmings of parsley, or the hard parts of asparagus—as all these have great nutrients. When the bag is full, empty the contents into a large pot and cover with water.

Add a piece of seaweed; 2 Tbsp apple cider vinegar, to draw out the calcium from the bones; and some salt and pepper, to taste.

Bring to a boil, then lower to a simmer; the broth can be simmered on the stove overnight if you desire. In the morning, let it cool, and then strain. Drink some at once, put some in the fridge, and freeze the rest in serving-size containers.

Now you have a very nourishing broth to drink and use for making soups. My friend Louise makes a large pot of this every week and drinks at least a cup a day.

Fish Chowder

3 Tbsp butter
1 cup leeks (which are more digestible than onions), chopped
2 cloves garlic, chopped
½ cup carrots, chopped

½ cup celery, chopped
½ cup potato, sweet potato, or yam, diced
2 cups chicken broth or vegetable stock
¼ cup parsley, chopped
Salt and pepper, to taste
1 cup white fish (halibut, cod, sole, bass, snapper, etc.), cut
  into cubes

Melt butter on low heat. Add vegetables and broth and simmer until tender. Add fish and simmer 3 more minutes. Garnish with chopped parsley or chives.

Note: A chopped tomato can be added to this chowder to make cioppino.

Easy Split Pea Soup

2 cups split peas, dried
3 Tbsp olive oil
1 onion, chopped
3 carrots, chopped
2 celery stalks, diced
2 Tbsp Coconut Aminos (soy-free seasoning sauce, available
  at: **www.coconutsecret.com**) or soy sauce
Ham bone
1 cup cooked ham, diced (optional)
1 bay leaf
Dash salt and pepper (may not need salt if ham is used)

Soak split peas overnight; drain and rinse well. Sauté onion in olive oil; add carrots and celery. Add split peas, ham bone, and flavorings, and cover with water. Choose a large pot—split peas swell in volume. Cook until peas are tender; add diced ham and simmer for 15 minutes. This soup can be pureed in the blender and always tastes better the next day after flavors have blended. Freezes well.

Note: Split peas can be very indigestible for some people. In addition, this soup is not low in carbohydrates.

Caroline's Famous Turkey Soup

After Thanksgiving and other holidays, my children always ask me for turkey soup. The flavor secret for this soup is leeks—a mild onion.

Remove all the remaining meat from a turkey carcass and set aside. Cover carcass with water and boil for 2 hours. Remove carcass; reserve liquid and meat pieces.

In a very large kettle, sauté 2 large leeks in 3 Tbsp turkey fat or olive oil. Add 4 stalks chopped celery and 2 chopped carrots. Add turkey stock, 2 vegetable bouillon cubes or pan drippings from roasted turkey, and additional water if needed. Add ½ cup barley. Simmer until vegetables are tender and barley is soft—about 1 hour. Add reserved turkey meat, a dash of lemon juice, and salt and pepper.

Note: In place of barley, use rice.

Carrot, Coconut, and Cumin Soup

3 Tbsp olive oil
10 large carrots, peeled and chopped
1 large onion, diced
2 cloves garlic, minced
1 tsp ginger, chopped
2 tsp cumin powder
1 veggie bouillon cube
8 cups water

2 oranges, juiced (cooked citrus can be less acidic)
1 tsp orange rind
1 cup coconut milk powder
Salt and pepper, to taste
2 Tbsp fresh parsley, chopped for garnish

Heat olive oil in a large soup pot. Sauté carrots, onion, garlic, and ginger; add water and bouillon cube and bring to a boil. Mix coconut milk powder with orange juice, orange rind, and cumin, until mixture is blended (may need additional water); add to soup pot. Simmer soup on medium heat until carrots are soft.

Blend soup with hand blender until smooth and creamy. Add salt and pepper to taste and sprinkle with fresh parsley.

Note: The addition of coconut milk makes a delicious, creamy soup without dairy products. This recipe can also be halved.

Potato and Dill Soup

3 Tbsp olive oil
6 large potatoes, quartered
2 cloves of garlic, minced
1 large onion, chopped
½ cup chopped fresh dill, or 3 Tbsp dried dill
½ cup white wine
6 cups boiling water
1 tsp balsamic vinegar
1 vegetable bouillon cube

Heat olive oil in a large soup kettle. Sauté garlic and onions until soft. Add potato, water, wine, bouillon cube, and balsamic vinegar; simmer until potatoes are completely soft. Blend soup with hand blender until smooth and creamy. Stir in fresh chopped dill, and simmer on low heat for an additional 5 minutes. Add salt and pepper to taste.

Note: A handful of cooked and chopped bacon, ham, smoked salmon, or smoked turkey is a tasty addition to this soup. And in place of potatoes, try yams or sweet potatoes.

Creamy Broccoli and Red Pepper Soup

3 Tbsp olive oil
2 cups broccoli florets, chopped
2 large red peppers, chopped
1 large white onion, minced
2 cloves garlic, minced
4 large potatoes, peeled and chopped
1 vegetable bouillon cube
½ cup coconut milk powder, or 1 can coconut milk
1 tsp dried basil
1 tsp curry powder
Juice of 1 lemon
1 tsp lemon rind, grated
½ cup fresh basil, chopped
8 cups boiling water
Salt and pepper to taste

Heat olive oil in a large soup pot. Sauté broccoli, onion, garlic, red pepper, and dried herbs until soft. Add potatoes, bouillon cube, water, coconut milk powder (blend first to remove lumps), lemon rind, lemon juice, and water; simmer until potatoes are soft. Blend with hand blender, and add salt and pepper to taste. Stir in fresh basil, and simmer soup for an additional 5–10 minutes.

Roasted Parsnip Soup

2 lbs parsnips, peeled
1 large yellow cooking onion
1 quart organic chicken stock
2 cloves garlic
2 Tbsp coconut oil
2 Tbsp olive oil
1 tsp cumin
¼ tsp salt

Preheat oven to 350° F.

Wash, peel, and cut parsnips; pat dry. Rub parsnips with coconut oil so that each side is coated. Place on a greased baking sheet and roast in the oven for 1–2 hours or until parsnips are tender. Sauté onion and garlic in olive oil; add chicken stock, cumin, and salt. Simmer until onion is tender. Add roasted parsnips and more stock if necessary. Blend in batches until creamy. Garnish with chopped chives.

Mary and Clark's Green Soup

I resisted this blended cold vegetable soup for years. Now I can't resist it! I use a handy Braun chopper and hand blender or a food processor for the prep work.

1 handful each of: kale, parsley, and spinach
2 cloves garlic (optional—I actually prefer this recipe without the garlic)
2 green onions (optional—some people prefer not to add green onion)
½ cup zucchini, grated
1 small organic cucumber, peeled
1 medium avocado
1 medium red or yellow sweet bell pepper

½ organic apple or pear, unpeeled
2 Tbsp Coconut Aminos (soy-free seasoning sauce, available
  at: **www.coconutsecret.com**)—optional

Chop the ingredients in a chopper container in 3 batches, then transfer to cylinder and blend until smooth with hand blender; or blend all ingredients together in the food processor. This mixture blends well depending on the size of your cucumber and avocado. You may need to add a little water to create a smooth consistency.

SNACKS & APPETIZERS

Because I live in a beautiful home with an ocean view, I love to share it with friends. The following are some of the items I have on hand for such occasions where I want to be festive but don't want to eat "off" my program. (I always have sparkling water in my refrigerator as well as assorted alcoholic drinks for my guests.)

First in this chapter are the appetizers my friends and I tend to enjoy; then my niece Georgia has contributed some of her favorites. I know you're going to want to try them all!

CAROLINE'S FAVORITE APPETIZERS

Smoked Salmon Butter

½ lb lox, smoked salmon, or barbeque smoked salmon tips
1 stick or ¼ lb butter

Blend in food processor till creamy. Serve with crispy rice crackers (available in any grocery store in the Asian specialty section), zucchini rounds, broccoli florets, or any raw vegetable.

Note: Smoked Salmon Butter is rich but extremely yummy. This recipe doubles and triples easily, and it freezes well, too.

Smoked Mussels and Smoked Oysters

I have these on hand and serve them on small slices of pumpernickel bread or crispy rice crackers, with a few capers.

Artichoke Dip

1 cup sheep pecorino cheese, grated
1 cup mayonnaise
1 cup plain (Greek style) goat yogurt
2 cups marinated artichoke hearts, drained and chopped
2 cloves garlic, minced
¼ cup fresh parsley, minced
¼ cup chives, finely chopped
⅓ cup roasted red peppers, drained and chopped

Preheat oven to 350° F.

Combine all ingredients and spread evenly into a buttered 8" baking dish. Top with roasted red pepper pieces. Bake 30 minutes or until heated through and bubbly. Serve with tamari rice crackers or my favorite—Lundberg Sesame & Seaweed rice chips, available at: **www.lundberg.com**.

Chips

Speaking of chips, you can serve a variety of potato chips, corn chips, or delicious vegetable chips or rice sticks, which are available at all health-food stores.

Roasted Nuts

Roasting nuts destroys mold. Place any variety that you want to roast on a baking sheet in a 250°–325° F oven for approximately 20 minutes to ½ hour or until golden brown. Watch pecans, as they burn quickly.

I always have a jar of toasted pine nuts on hand, because they are great to sprinkle on a salad or jazz up an hors d'oeuvre platter. Place a couple of handfuls of pine nuts in a cast iron skillet. Turn the heat on medium low, stirring frequently until golden brown. Cool and store in a glass jar. Refrigerate.

Nut Butters

Serve a variety of nut butters—cashew butter, almond butter, or a combination of cashew and macadamia nut butter. These are available at any health-food store. You can also make your own by roasting nuts and blending them in a hand blender till creamy. Add salt if desired.

Nut Butter Balls

I am grateful to my friend Dawn Landon, nutritional consultant and health coach, for her variations on a simple theme.

Nut Butter Balls make a quick and nutritious snack—in fact, my hairdresser has them on hand for a quick energy fix between clients when she has little time to sit down for lunch.

Mix equal portions of warmed nut butter (almond butter or cashew butter work well) and coconut oil*. Place the mixture in the fridge until firm enough to work with. With a small melon scoop, create balls out of the mixture and roll in fine shredded coconut. Store in a covered container in the fridge.

Variation: Add 2–4 Tbsp hemp granules (high protein) to the nut butter and coconut oil mixture.

* I am not a big fan of microwave ovens, but in order to warm the nut butter and coconut oil, place the open container in a microwave for 30 seconds. You can also put the container in a double boiler on very low heat, or place it in the sun for ½ hour.

GEORGIA'S GREAT SNACKS

Ginger and Garlic Roasted Nuts

½ cup cashews
½ cup pecans
½ cup almonds
2 Tbsp ginger, minced and peeled
2 garlic cloves, minced
2 Tbsp tamari
Sea salt and cracked black pepper, to taste

Preheat oven to 325° F.
   In a bowl, coat nuts with mixture. Place nuts on a baking sheet in the oven for 15–20 minutes, until golden brown.

Red Pepper Dip

4 red bell peppers
Juice of 1 lemon
½ cup plain goat yogurt
1 Tbsp mayonnaise
2 cloves garlic, raw or roasted

1 tsp Dijon mustard
1 Tbsp capers

Preheat oven to 350° F.

Place peppers on a baking sheet and roast in the oven until most of the skin is black or charred. Take peppers out of the oven and place into an airtight plastic bag for 20 minutes. When peppers have cooled, peel off the burnt skin, remove seeds, and chop peppers coarsely. Add all ingredients together in the food processor and blend until creamy; add salt and pepper to taste. Serve with freshly cut vegetables

Nutty Lentil Pâté

2 cups red lentils, cooked
1 medium onion, diced
2 garlic cloves, minced
½ cup vegetable or chicken stock
2 tsp each—dried basil, oregano, and dill
½ cup pecans or walnuts, toasted
½ tsp chili flakes
1 Tbsp olive oil

In a medium pan, heat oil and sauté garlic and onion until soft. Add lentils, stock, and herbs. Allow the mixture to cook approximately 15 minutes, until most of the water has been absorbed and lentil mixture is thickened. Set aside to cool.

Blend nuts, chili flakes, and lemon juice in food processor; add mixture to cooled lentils. Garnish with chopped parsley, fresh basil, or dill. Serve with vegetables, apple slices, crispy rice crackers, or alternative bread.

Note: Not low in carbohydrates.

Artichoke-Heart Dip

1 can artichoke hearts, chopped coarsely
2 Tbsp mayonnaise
1 cup plain goat yogurt
Juice of 1 lemon
2 Tbsp freshly chopped dill, or 1 Tbsp dried dill
1 tsp grainy/coarse mustard
A few dashes of Worcestershire sauce
A few dashes of spicy hot sauce

Preheat oven to 350° F.

Combine all ingredients in an ovenproof bowl and heat in the oven for about 15 minutes, until dip is warmed through. Serve with freshly cut vegetables.

Guacamole

4 ripe avocados
2 Tbsp cilantro, chopped
Juice of 1 lime or lemon
⅓ red onion, minced
Sea salt and cracked black pepper, to taste

Mix ingredients together and serve immediately with freshly cut vegetables, strips of grilled chicken, and assorted chips or crackers.

Note: Add ½ cup sun-dried tomatoes, 1 Tbsp roasted garlic, a little cumin, or hot sauce to guacamole for added zest.

Smoked Salmon Rolls

½ lb smoked salmon, thinly sliced
2 tsp horseradish
2 Tbsp mayonnaise
1 Tbsp capers, chopped
Juice of 1 lemon
2 Tbsp fresh dill, chopped
Sea salt and cracked black pepper, to taste

Mix horseradish, mayonnaise, capers, and lemon juice together. Lay each smoked salmon slice out flat and spread with a small amount of the mixture. Carefully roll up each slice, and dip one end into freshly chopped dill. Serve like a fan on an attractive plate. Garnish with lemon wedges.

Deviled Eggs

Hard-boil any number of free-range eggs; run under cold water to cool. Cut eggs in half; spoon out yolks and mash with a fork. Add mayonnaise to form a firm but creamy mixture, and spoon back into the egg halves. Sprinkle with salt, pepper, and paprika.

Variation: Add 1–2 tsp Dijon mustard, chopped jalapeño, parsley, dill, or fresh chive.

Note: These are great to have on hand for snacking.

Hummus

1 can garbanzo beans, drained
2 cloves garlic, raw or roasted
Juice of 1 lemon

2 tsp olive oil
1–3 Tbsp tahini paste (sesame-seed butter)
1 tsp dried chili flakes
Salt and pepper, to taste

Put all ingredients in a food processor and whiz until creamy in texture. Serve with freshly cut vegetables, crispy rice crackers, or appropriate chips.

Note: Not low in carbohydrates.

Cherry Tomatoes Filled with Hummus and Olive Spread

24 cherry tomatoes, with the tops cut out and seeds removed

Olive Spread:
1 can kalamata olives, pitted
2 cloves garlic, minced
Juice of 1 lemon
½ cup fresh parsley, chopped
1 tsp cayenne pepper
Salt and pepper, to taste

Combine all ingredients in the food processor and blend lightly.

Fill each cherry tomato with hummus (see recipe above) and top with a small amount of tapenade (olive spread).

Easy Mini Pizzas

4 slices 100 percent rye* bread, appetizer-size pumpernickel bread, rice bread, or any non-gluten bread—toasted and left out to dry

¼ cup sun-dried tomatoes or roasted red pepper pieces
4–8 slices sheep or goat cheese, enough to cover bread
1 Tbsp fresh basil, finely chopped
¼ cup olive oil

Preheat oven to 350° F.

Brush baking sheet with olive oil; brush bread with olive oil and place on baking sheet. Cover bread with sun-dried tomato or red peppers, and add cheese slices. Garnish with several small pieces of red pepper or tomato. Sprinkle with minced basil and drizzle with remaining olive oil.

Bake 10–15 minutes or until top is bubbly and golden brown. Serves 2–4, depending on bread size.

* Rye contains a minimal amount of gluten. If you are celiac, do not use 100 percent rye products. This is not a low-carb recipe.

———————————————————

DINNER

I like to keep things simple. After years of cooking "three squares" a day for a family, I do not relish the thought of slaving over a hot stove—ever! I prefer to plan ahead and purchase items full of protein that I can eat and enjoy as leftovers the next day. I love fish, and since it's plentiful on the West Coast, that makes it a good choice for me. In the summer there is nothing easier to prepare than avocado and shrimp on a bed of butter lettuce.

A favorite in colder weather (or anytime) is leg of lamb—roasted very slowly in the oven. There's nothing better than cold roast lamb for several dinners. A large pan of pork chops or combo meatballs will keep me stocked. While it's not everyone's choice, I find that many people thrive on red meat.

I make a small salad for dinner and a huge amount of steamed vegetables. Often I will have a small amount of baked squash, steamed sweet potato or yam, or parsnip hash browns as a starch choice. This kind of dinner makes me happy.

During my presentations I am always aware of busy people—including single parents, working moms, elderly folks, and others who don't have a lot of time or desire to cook. Consequently, I recommend the use of a slow cooker or a tabletop grill for just about everyone.

A tabletop grill is about the size of a tennis racquet and

sits at an angle on the kitchen counter so that the fat from the meat drips down into a container below the grill. Here's the best way to use it:

- Place any meat, poultry, or fish, you wish to cook on the surface of the hot grill—chicken breasts, turkey sausages, steak, or lamb chops work well. Brush the surface of the meat with soy sauce, garlic salt, or Coconut Aminos, and sprinkle with herbs or spices. Then arrange cut-up vegetables next to the meat—such as eggplant slices, zucchini strips, or peppers. Brush vegetables with vinaigrette dressing or olive oil.

- After 10–15 minutes, turn the meat over and grill the other side. Remove the vegetables. Serve this meal with any appropriate starch or carbohydrate of your choice (or if you are doing low carb, no starch).

A slow cooker also works very well and is a lazy way to prepare an evening meal in the morning. Here's how:

- Take any sort of meat you wish to cook. Chicken, turkey, or beef works well; and lamb shanks are wonderfully tasty cooked this way. Place the meat in the slow cooker and add approximately 2 cups of water, stock, or chicken or beef broth. Season to taste with salt, pepper, fresh herbs, or non-fermented soy sauce. Add 1 chopped onion, 2 chopped celery stalks, and 1 chopped carrot.

- Turn on the slow cooker and leave to simmer for the day. Eight hours later, you will return to delicious smells and an inviting meal. Cook a pot of rice or a baked potato, fix a quick salad, and voilà! The evening meal is prepared *and* there are plenty of leftovers.

ROASTS & STEAK

Greek-Style Pork or Lamb Roast

2–3 lbs pork or lamb roast
2 Tbsp roasted garlic
Juice of 1 lemon
1 onion, minced
1 tsp oregano
1 tsp thyme
1 tsp rosemary (for lamb)
2 baking potatoes, unpeeled and cut into wedges
2 carrots, peeled and cut into wedges
1½ cups water
1 beef bouillon cube

In a medium-size skillet, brown the roast on all sides with a small amount of olive oil. Place the roast into the slow cooker and arrange the other ingredients around it. Pour in water and crumbled bouillon cube. Turn slow cooker to medium and heat the roast. Then adjust the temperature and continue cooking for 6–8 hours on simmer. Serve with salad and fresh steamed vegetables.

Variation: A 3-lb leg of lamb, placed in a covered casserole or roasting pan with: 1 onion, quartered; 2 carrots and 2 celery sticks, chopped; 2 cloves garlic, chopped; and a handful of fresh rosemary scattered over the roast. Cook at 325° F till roast sizzles, then lower the heat to 200° for 2–3 hours or until meat is very tender—my favorite.

Marinated Skirt Steak

3 lbs skirt steak, round steak, or simmering steak, marinated
3 baby potatoes, per person

Marinade:
½ cup tamari, soy sauce, or Bragg Liquid Aminos
2 Tbsp garlic, roasted or raw
1 cup water
1 Tbsp hoisin sauce
1 Tbsp Dijon mustard

Place the steak in the marinade for at least 24 hours. Remove meat from marinade and brown in a skillet on all sides with a small amount of olive oil. Place meat in slow cooker and pour the remaining marinade plus ½ cup water over the meat. Cook at medium setting for 6–8 hours. (Heat may be reduced after several hours.) In the last hour, add potatoes or steam them separately for 15 minutes.

Note: A slow cooker is not a good way to preserve nutrients in vegetables because of the length of cooking. Be sure to include a couple of steamed or grilled vegetables along with your slow-cooker meals.

Caroline's Christmas Ham

Even though hams are cured and precooked, there is nothing better than a ham that is cooked through again, which is why everyone loves this recipe. The secret is to cook the ham low and slow—this keeps the meat moist and tender and allows it to slice easily. This is a party pleaser at a seasonal "open house." Serve with a selection of alternative breads, a large basket of curly leaf lettuce, big bowls of sliced sweet pickles, mayonnaise, and creamy Dijon mustard.

1 whole organic ham or butt end with the bone in—do *not* choose a presliced ham for this recipe
2 Tbsp hot *dry* (powdered) mustard (Colman's is best)

Preheat oven to 400° F.

Place ham in a large open roasting pan and rub all over with dry mustard. Score skin in a crisscross pattern and stud with cloves. Bake until ham starts to sizzle; immediately turn down the oven to 200° for 5–8 hours—low and slow. You may want to place a loose tent of aluminum foil over the ham as it cooks at the low temperature. Make sure the air can circulate around the ham, which will help keep it from drying out.

Note: After the meat is all eaten, save the ham bone for Easy Split Pea Soup. See recipe in the soup section.

MEATBALLS (GREAT "BALLS" OF PROTEIN)

If you're packing a lunch, need to travel, or just grabbing a snack on the run, the following meatball recipes are delicious and handy, and they make great leftovers.

Turkey Meatballs

2 stalks celery, finely chopped
1 medium carrot, finely chopped
1 tsp "Spike" herbal seasoning mix (available at health-food stores)
1 lb ground turkey
1 Tbsp Bragg Liquid Aminos, Coconut Aminos (soy-free seasoning sauce, available at: **www.coconutsecret.com**), or soy sauce

Combine chopped celery, carrots, and Spike; sauté in 1 tbsp olive oil until soft. Mix aminos or soy sauce and ground turkey; add cooked celery and carrots. Form mixture into balls and fry in olive oil until golden brown.

These are great for breakfast or any meal, as well as a hot or cold snack. They travel well in an insulated bag, and freeze well, too. Kids will love them—my grandchildren certainly do!

Turkey Pan Squares

Follow the Turkey Meatball recipe above, but for a variation, press the mixture into a buttered 8"-square glass baking dish. Bake at 350° F for 1 hour; when cool, cut into squares. Freeze and add a couple of squares to morning veggies or carry to work in an insulated bag.

Optional: Coat the top with organic, low-sugar ketchup before baking.

Combo Meatballs

½ lb each: ground lamb, pork, and beef
1–2 Tbsp Coconut Aminos (soy-free seasoning sauce, available at: **www.coconutsecret.com**)
2 tsp Jordanian Roast Lamb Spice (I love this for lamb—it's available at: **www.spicebazaar.com** or by calling: 1-800-30-SPICE)

Combine ingredients and form into balls; sprinkle with a little more Jordanian Spice. Fry in olive oil until golden brown, or form into patties and barbeque.

These are great hot or cold, dipped in creamy Dijon mustard.

Robust Tomato Sauce and Meatballs

1 can stewed tomatoes
2 fresh tomatoes, diced
½ can tomato paste
1 clove garlic, minced
½ tsp sugar
1 carrot, peeled and chopped
1 Tbsp mixed Italian seasoning (dried oregano, basil, thyme)

1½ cups cold water
Salt and pepper, to taste
Chili flakes, if you want a little spice

Combine ingredients and simmer on medium heat for approximately 45 minutes. When the sauce is cooked, use a hand mixer to puree sauce.

Traditional Meatballs

2 lbs lean ground beef or ground turkey
1 clove garlic, minced
2 Tbsp chickpea flour (an optional binder and legume available in East Indian markets) or rice flour
1 egg, beaten
Salt and pepper, to taste
2 tsp oregano flakes
2 tsp basil flakes

Combine all ingredients and form into small balls. Cook in hot olive oil until golden brown. Serve with tomato sauce and non-wheat pasta or spaghetti squash.

Note: Remember, many people are sensitive to tomatoes due to their high acidity. Give tomatoes a break for a while and you should be able to tolerate them on an occasional basis.

Instead of tomato sauce, add ⅓ cup chicken stock, water, and vegetable bouillon cube or Coconut Aminos to pan drippings. Thicken with arrowroot powder or rice flour to make gravy. For a sweet-and-sour taste, add ⅓ cup chopped pineapple to the gravy.

Tangy Ginger Coconut Meatballs

1 lb ground beef, lamb, or turkey
1 egg
1 tsp garlic, minced
1 tsp hot mustard
1 tsp gingerroot, minced
1 Tbsp Coconut Aminos (soy-free seasoning sauce, available
   at: **www.coconutsecret.com**)

Mix ingredients together and form into balls. Cook over medium heat until golden brown. Set aside and keep warm.

Tangy Sauce:
½ cup coconut milk
½ cup vegetable or chicken stock
2 tsp orange or lemon juice
2 tsp minced garlic
2 tsp fresh ginger
2 tsp grated orange rind

Mix sauce ingredients together in a small saucepan and gently simmer for 15 minutes, stirring frequently. Pour over warm meatballs.

Yummy Lamb Patties

1 lb ground lamb
1 tsp Jordanian Roast Lamb Spice (available at:
   www.spicebazaar.com or by calling: 1-800-30-SPICE)
¼ lb goat chèvre cheese
2 Tbsp fresh rosemary

Form ground lamb into thin patties. Sprinkle each patty with Jordanian Roast Lamb Spice and press the outside of each patty into fresh rosemary. Sandwich a generous blob of goat chèvre between two meat patties. Press together. Cook on tabletop grill or barbeque for approximately 5–10 minutes per side. (It's great cold, too.)

Optional: Omit the goat cheese.

FISH

Please note that some of these recipes call for lemon and lemon rind—when these items are cooked, they are less acidic. If you are legume sensitive, know that tamari or soy sauce will cause problems only in rare cases. But do omit any ingredients you do not feel comfortable using.

Salmon

To me there is nothing nicer than a fillet of fresh salmon, pan-fried in a little butter and a squeeze of lemon.
My variations:

1. Chop fresh ginger very finely; heat in 1 Tbsp melted butter. Lightly coat fillet with tamari sauce (wheat-free soy sauce) and place skin-side up in butter and ginger. Turn over when browned and squeeze fresh lemon on top. Continue cooking, approximately 5 minutes till cooked through.

2. Cook salmon fillet, then liberally coat with real mayonnaise and sprinkle with fresh or dried dill. Place under broiler until mayonnaise is browned and bubbly. This is great cold.

3. For a party favorite, place a whole side of salmon on heavy-duty foil and slather the entire piece of fish with mayonnaise and dill. Leave foil open and barbeque for about 15 minutes or until cooked through. Or bake in the oven at 400° F—but add some water to the pan as the salmon can smoke or flare up. Ovens can be very messy!

Here's my niece Georgia's own variation:

Basil Mayonnaise for Salmon
One (6 oz) salmon fillet or steak, per person
1 cup real mayonnaise
½ cup fresh basil, chopped
The juice of 1 lemon
Rind of 1 lemon, finely grated
Salt and pepper, to taste

Preheat oven to 350° F.
Combine all ingredients and spread over each salmon fillet or steak before baking. Bake fish for 20–25 minutes until the top is slightly golden brown. May use broiler to complete browning. Serve fish with lemon wedges and chopped parsley.

Mushroom Red Wine Sauce

One (6 oz) salmon fillet, per person
2 cups mushrooms, sliced
2 cloves garlic, crushed and minced
½ cup fresh parsley, chopped
3 carrots, peeled and grated
2 celery stalks, diced
½ cup real mayonnaise
2 Tbsp tapioca starch or arrowroot powder
1 cup cold water
⅓ cup red wine

Salt and pepper, to taste

Preheat oven to 350° F.

Sauté mushrooms, garlic, parsley, carrots, and celery until soft. Combine water, tapioca starch, and mayonnaise; whisk together until blended. Add starch mixture to the mushroom mixture and allow to thicken. Simmer for a few minutes; add wine, salt, and pepper.

Place salmon in a baking dish and cover with the mushroom sauce. Place in the oven and bake for 20–25 minutes. Serve warm.

Note: Mushrooms are part of the mold/fungus family. Even if you are following a Candida-eradication program, however, mushrooms may be eaten occasionally.

Baked Sole with Lemon, Capers, and Toasted Pine Nuts

One or two (4–6 oz) sole fillets, per person
1 tsp olive oil
Juice of 1 lemon
Rind of 1 lemon (can be omitted)
3 Tbsp chopped capers
1 tsp dried dill or 1 Tbsp fresh dill, chopped
½ cup pine nuts, toasted 5 minutes in a small frying pan

Preheat oven to 350° F.

In a small mixing bowl, combine olive oil, lemon juice, lemon rind, capers, and dill. Spread the mixture over the sole fillets and sprinkle a few pine nuts in the middle of each fillet. Roll the fillets up tightly and sprinkle with salt and pepper to taste. Bake for 15 minutes. Do not overcook this fish—it is delicate and beautiful when cooked minimally.

Black Bean Cod

One (6 oz) cod fillet, per person
1 can black beans, rinsed
Juice of 1 lemon
Juice of 1 lime
1 onion, minced
3 cloves garlic, minced
2 Tbsp cilantro, chopped
1 tsp chili flakes (optional)

Preheat oven to 350° F.

Combine all ingredients in a shallow baking dish and coat the fish. Bake until fish is flaky in the middle—approximately 15 minutes. Garnish with fresh chopped cilantro.

Red Snapper with Black Olives

One (6 oz) snapper fillet, per person
½ red onion, minced
3 garlic cloves, minced
1 large red bell pepper, slivered
1 cup kalamata olives, pitted (or canned black olives)
4 Tbsp capers
½ cup dry red wine
1 tsp chili flakes
Lemon juice
Sea salt and cracked black pepper, to taste

Preheat oven to 350° F.

In a large skillet, heat 2 Tbsp olive oil to medium heat. Add onion, garlic, olives, and capers; sauté until soft and the flavors are blended. Add red wine, chili flakes, lemon juice, and salt and pepper to taste.

Place fish in a baking dish and brush with olive oil. Cook for 5–10 minutes, or until fish is soft and flaky—no more than 15 minutes. Pour hot sauce over fish and garnish with fresh parsley and lemon wedges.

Halibut with Toasted Pecans and Fresh Spinach Pesto

One (6 oz) halibut steak, per person
½ cup fresh tarragon, chopped
1 bunch fresh spinach, trimmed and washed
Juice of 1 lemon
Sea salt and cracked black pepper, to taste
½ cup toasted pecans

Preheat oven to 350° F.
Place halibut in a shallow baking dish with 2 Tbsp water. Bake for 20 minutes.
While the fish is cooking prepare the pesto: In a food processor, blend olive oil, tarragon, spinach, and lemon juice. Add salt and pepper to taste. When the fish is cooked, place 1 Tbsp pesto on top of each steak. Garnish with toasted pecans.

Crusted Tuna Steak

One (6 oz) tuna steak, per person
Cracked black peppercorns
½ cup tamari
½ Tbsp sesame oil
½ cup white wine
3 Tbsp gingerroot, chopped finely
2 Tbsp sesame seeds
2 Tbsp fresh cilantro, chopped
Juice of 1 lime

Salt and pepper, to taste

Turn barbecue on to medium heat.

Coat each tuna steak with cracked black peppercorns and a little salt. Grill on the BBQ or panfry on both sides. Tuna steaks are very nice cooked quite rare—or well done as desired.

Sauté the ginger root in the sesame oil (or any oil) with lime juice, white wine, and tamari; simmer until the sauce reduces slightly. Pour a little sauce over each tuna steak. Garnish with sesame seeds and chopped cilantro.

Crab and Shrimp Cakes with Sweet Pepper Sauce

1 lb fresh crabmeat (imitation crab also works well), cooked
1 lb fresh shrimp, cooked
2 Tbsp real mayonnaise
1 cup rice crackers or rice cakes, ground
1 tsp cumin
1 tsp curry powder
1 Tbsp chopped capers
1 garlic clove, minced
½ red onion, minced
Salt and pepper, to taste

Combine all ingredients and shape into small cakes. Lightly fry each cake until golden brown on both sides.

Sweet Pepper Sauce:
2 red peppers, minced
1 tsp ginger, minced
1 tsp olive oil
Juice of 1 orange
2 Tbsp water

Sauté red pepper with olive oil and ginger. Add orange juice and water; reduce until slightly thickened. Drizzle sauce over top of cakes and serve on a bed of lettuce greens.

Note: This sauce is also delicious with chicken.

Prawn Kebabs with Fresh Kiwi or Papaya Salsa

2 lbs raw prawns, peeled and deveined
1 red onion, cut into chunks
Juice of 1 lemon
1 tsp paprika
2 garlic cloves, minced
Salt and pepper, to taste

Marinate prawns in the lemon juice, paprika, salt, and pepper for about 20 minutes. Spear prawns and onion chunks onto kebabs or skewer sticks. Grill for 2–3 minutes on each side.

Salsa:
3 kiwifruits, peeled and chopped; or 1 whole papaya, peeled, seeded, and chopped (or both)
Juice of 1 lime
2 Tbsp cilantro, chopped
2 Tbsp parsley, chopped
2 cloves garlic, minced

Combine all ingredients for 5 minutes to allow flavors to blend together. Serve salsa on a decorated platter, beside kebabs.

POULTRY

Surprisingly, many people have sensitivities to chicken. It can give them gas and even put them to sleep! Try organic chicken, capon, Cornish game hen, or turkey as alternatives to the following recipes.

Lemon Chicken

1 boneless chicken breast, per person
1 Tbsp rice flour
1 clove garlic, minced
1 cup water
Juice and rind of 2 lemons
1 Tbsp arrowroot powder
Salt and pepper, to taste
½ cup roasted almonds, slivered

Preheat oven to 400° F.

Lightly dust each chicken breast in rice flour. Sauté garlic in olive or cold-pressed vegetable oil until soft; add lemon juice and rind. Combine cold water with the arrowroot powder until blended, and add to lemon mixture. Allow sauce to thicken adding a little more water if needed.

Place chicken breasts in pan with sauce. Cover and bake for 25 minutes—uncover for the last 10 minutes. Garnish with roasted, slivered almonds.

Orange Roasted Chicken

2–4 lbs roasting chicken
1 Tbsp butter
1 tsp dried sage
1 tsp dried marjoram
1 tsp dried thyme
Juice of 2 fresh oranges—reserve the peel
1 tsp salt
Preheat oven to 400° F.

Pat chicken dry with paper towels and place in a covered roasting pan. Rub chicken all over with butter and sprinkle with salt and dried herbs. Squeeze orange juice over chicken and poke the orange peels into chicken cavity. Roast covered for 1 hour; remove lid and continue to bake for 15–20 minutes.

Serve with baked butternut or kabocha squash wedges, which can bake alongside the chicken inside or outside of the roasting pan.

BBQ Chicken with Coconut Cashew Sauce

1 chicken breast, per person (can also use legs or thighs)
Salt and pepper

Coconut Cashew Sauce:
½ cup coconut milk
1 Tbsp white wine vinegar
1 Tbsp ketchup
Juice of 1 lime
1 cup cashews, ground
¼ cup whole roasted cashews

Combine all ingredients in a pan and allow to reduce on low heat for 5–10 minutes.

Barbeque the chicken on foil or cook on a tabletop grill for 15 minutes or until the meat is tender. Spoon warm sauce over chicken, and add toasted cashews for garnish.

Mustard Chicken

1 boneless chicken breast, per person
1 egg, beaten
½ cup rice flour, with a dash of salt and pepper mixed in
3 Tbsp olive oil
1 clove garlic, minced
½ cup mayonnaise
⅓ cup cold water
1½ Tbsp tapioca starch
½ cup chopped parsley
⅓ cup grainy/coarse Dijon mustard
Salt and pepper, to taste

Dip each chicken breast in the beaten egg and coat with rice-flour mixture. Shake off excess flour.

Heat oil in frying pan on medium heat; add garlic and sauté until soft. In a small bowl, combine mayonnaise, water, tapioca starch, parsley, and Dijon mustard; whisk until smooth and blended. Pour mayonnaise mixture into the pan with the garlic and allow to simmer and thicken slightly.

In another pan, heat a little oil and cook the chicken for 5 minutes on each side or until cooked. Pour the warm Dijon sauce over chicken breasts and serve.

Tuscan Chicken Marinade

1 cup red wine vinegar
1 clove garlic, minced
1 cup frozen raspberries, cooked and pureed

½ cup olive oil
Salt and pepper, to taste

Combine all ingredients and cover chicken breasts with mixture. Marinate 1 hour or longer—overnight is best. Grill, fry, barbeque, or bake this chicken.

Asian Marinade for Chicken

2 Tbsp tamari
2 Tbsp hoisin sauce
1 clove garlic, minced
1 tsp powdered ginger; or 1 Tbsp fresh gingerroot, chopped
    and peeled

Combine all ingredients and allow chicken to marinate for 1 hour or longer. This marinade is perfect for baking or barbequing. Grill chicken approximately 8 minutes on each side, or bake 35 minutes in a 350° F oven. Serve with a dusting of toasted sesame seeds.

Yummy Macaroni and Cheese, with Chicken

½ lb rice or quinoa elbow macaroni, cooked and drained
2 cups rice chips, crushed—set aside for topping

Sauce:
3 Tbsp butter
¼ cup onion, finely chopped (optional)
¼ cup spelt flour
3 cups rice milk
2 cups sheep pecorino cheese, grated
1 cup mild chèvre goat cheese log
⅓ cup pecorino cheese—reserve for topping

1 cup cherry tomatoes
3 cups cooked chicken breasts or leftover chicken, cubed
Pinch of salt, pepper, and cayenne pepper
⅛ tsp nutmeg

Preheat oven to 375° F degrees.

Cook pasta according to package directions; drain and set aside. Place rice chips in a heavy plastic bag and crush with a rolling pin; set aside.

To prepare cheese sauce: Melt butter in a 4-quart pot over medium heat. Add onion and cook, stirring occasionally, until translucent—about 5 minutes. Add flour and cook, stirring with a wooden spoon, until bubbling but not brown. Add rice milk slowly and stir to combine. Bring to a simmer, stirring frequently with a wooden spoon until thick —about 5 minutes. Add pecorino and chèvre cheeses, stirring until completely melted and sauce is smooth. Season with salt and pepper; add cayenne and nutmeg, and stir well.

Add rice pasta to cheese sauce and stir well. Slowly add cherry tomatoes and chicken cubes and combine. Pour into buttered casserole dish; sprinkle with reserved pecorino cheese and top with rice-chip crumbs.

Bake 45 minutes to 1 hour or until bubbly and brown on top. Serves 4–6 people.

Note: As you can imagine, this dish is not low in carbohydrates.

Accompaniments

In my own quest for health, there have been two distinct parts of the journey. The first milestone was when I learned that "offending foods" had a direct effect on my health. But the second and most dramatic level of wellness occurred when I vastly reduced my carbohydrate intake, even the so-called healthy carbs.

This section will give you some ideas on how to assuage your own starch desires. As you'll see, wild rice, millet, quinoa, sweet potatoes, yams, and many other interesting grains and root vegetables are good choices to help you wean yourself off of wheat, potatoes, and pasta at dinnertime.

Parsnip Hash Browns

This is a favorite of mine. When parsnips are cooked, they have a sweet, nutty taste.

Grate 1 cup parsnips (washed and unpeeled), and melt 1½ Tbsp butter or clarified butter in a small frying pan.

Add parsnips to melted butter and cook 5 minutes on medium heat until edges are brown and sizzling. Gently turn parsnips over with a large lifter and cook the other side. Sprinkle with salt and pepper, and serve.

Note: This dish has 10 carbohydrate grams.

Clarified Butter (Ghee):

Place 1 lb butter in a small heavy pan. Slowly simmer until butter is melted—about 1 hour. Skim foam off the top (milk solids); pour the remaining clear yellow liquid into a wide-mouthed glass jar. Be careful not to add the whey and milk solids from the bottom of the pan, and cap the jar. This butter will keep indefinitely in the refrigerator.

Note: Clarified butter is wonderful for cooking because it does not spatter and burn; it is also easy to melt for steamed asparagus or other vegetables and has a variety of other uses. In addition, it is great for people with dairy allergies because the milk solids have been removed.

Louise Hay's Roasted Vegetables

Assemble equal amounts (more or less) of the following vegetables:

- Celery
- Parsnips
- Turnips
- Rutabaga
- Carrots
- Potatoes
- Onions

Gather seasonings, such as clove, thyme, rosemary, salt, and pepper
A dab of butter or olive oil
Preheat oven to 350° F.
Quarter the onions and stud with cloves; cut the rest of the vegetables into small chunks. Mix together and sprinkle with

thyme, rosemary, salt, and pepper to taste. Place in a roasting pan and dot with butter or olive oil (butter tastes better).

Place in the oven, and just let it cook for a couple of hours until the vegetables are soft and almost caramelized.

Linda's Crispy Sesame Crusted Brussels Sprouts

6 Tbsp butter
3 Tbsp toasted sesame oil
3 Tbsp olive oil
1½ lbs Brussels sprouts, halved
½ tsp crushed red pepper (optional)
Dash of salt and pepper
3 Tbsp sesame seeds

In large skillet, melt butter in sesame oil and olive oil over medium heat; add Brussels sprouts, crushed red pepper, salt, and pepper. Cook, stirring frequently, until golden brown—about 25 minutes. Sprinkle sesame seeds on top and cook until the Brussels sprouts are dark brown and crunchy—about 15 minutes. Serve hot!

Beet Patties

This is an unusual accompaniment to a dinner meal.

Grate 1 fresh beet (washed, unpeeled). Heat 1½ Tbsp clarified butter in a small frying pan.

Mix beet together with 1 beaten egg and a pinch of salt and pepper; spoon into hot butter. Turn when edges are crispy, and cook the other side.

Note: 1 cup beets = 12 carbohydrate grams.

Squashes

The choices of winter squash, a delicious and easily digestible accompaniment to your evening meal, are endless. Look for these types: banana; butternut; Danish; acorn; spaghetti; hubbard; or, my favorite, kabocha.

Here's how to prepare your squash: Split into halves or quarters. Bake in the oven with butter, salt and pepper, or cinnamon for approximately ½ hour at 350° F. Or cut into cubes and steam for less than 10 minutes.

Never add sugar to squash—it is sweet enough without added sugars.

Millet Stuffing

1 part millet
2 parts water
3 Tbsp clarified butter or olive oil
1 medium onion, chopped
1 Tbsp poultry spice

Rinse millet well and cook like rice—about 15 minutes or until just slightly crunchy.

While millet is cooking, sauté onion in a heavy frying pan until golden brown. Add poultry spice with onions until mixed well. Transfer desired amount of millet and fold into onion mixture. Add salt and pepper to taste.

Note: This works well with the addition of walnuts and celery as a turkey stuffing—move over "Stove Top"! Leftover plain millet can be reheated as a breakfast with alternative milk or coconut milk, and a handful of almonds or cashews. Leftover plain millet can also be made into a delicious tabouleh (see next recipe).

Millet Tabouleh

2–4 cups millet, cooked
3 green onions, chopped
1 green bell pepper, chopped
1 stalk celery, chopped
½ cup toasted almonds, chopped
¼ cup parsley, chopped
¼ cup fresh mint, chopped
1 large clove garlic, minced
6 Tbsp lemon juice
8 Tbsp olive oil

Mix garlic, olive oil, and vinegar in a small bowl; mix all other ingredients in a large bowl. Add dressing and stir till mixed well. Garnish with fresh parsley and mint.

Note: This is not low in carbohydrates (approximately 20 grams per cup).

Easy Corn Bread

¾ cup cornmeal
1 cup corn flour (available in health-food stores)
3 tsp baking powder
¾ tsp salt
2 Tbsp melted butter or ghee
4 Tbsp honey
1 cup rice milk
1 egg, beaten well

Preheat oven to 425° F.

Mix together dry ingredients. Melt honey with ghee in a small pan; add milk and egg. Combine wet and dry ingredients. Bake in a buttered 8″ x 8″ baking pan for 20 minutes.

Note: This dish is at its very best when eaten warm, right out of the oven. It will dry out by the next day, so reheat wrapped in a moist paper towel. (There are about 20 grams of carbohydrate per corn-bread chunk.)

Soda Bread

2 cups flour—rye, millet, rice, amaranth, or combination (rye works especially well)
1½ tsp baking powder
¼ tsp baking soda
1 cup water or milk

Preheat oven to 350° F.

Combine dry ingredients; add liquid to make a soft dough. Place on a lightly floured board and knead for one minute. Shape into a round loaf and place on an oiled baking sheet. Cut a "V" across the top with a sharp knife so that the bread can breathe and bake evenly. Bake 40–60 minutes, until loaf sounds slightly hollow when tapped.

Note: Add a handful of toasted sunflower seeds, flaxseeds, toasted walnuts, mashed banana, or grated carrot to the dough for variation. (There are 25 grams of carbohydrate per medium slice.)

Bacon Kasha

1 part whole buckwheat (kasha)
2 parts water
Salt to taste
4–6 strips cooked bacon or turkey bacon, crumbled
½ cup walnut pieces
1 medium onion, chopped

2 Tbsp wheat-free tamari or soy sauce
3 Tbsp olive oil

Rinse and pick over whole buckwheat. Drop into briskly boiling, salted water; simmer for 15 minutes or until just slightly crunchy to the taste. Don't overcook buckwheat or it will become mushy.

Cook bacon until crisp; crumble and reserve. Fry onion in olive oil; add crumbled bacon and walnut pieces. Add desired amount of cooked buckwheat. Stir well over medium heat so all ingredients are mixed. Add tamari 1 Tbsp at a time and check for flavor.

Note: This dish is not low in carbohydrates. Also, buckwheat is a separate grain related to rhubarb and not a wheat (see food families in the back of this book). Personally, I find it has an odd taste that has few redeeming features, unless it is masked in a savory dish like this one.

Wild-Rice Pancakes

4 cups wild rice, cooked
1 egg
½ cup rice flour
½ tsp baking powder
1 garlic clove, minced
1 tsp peeled ginger, minced
½ onion, minced (can be omitted)
1 tsp Dijon mustard
3 Tbsp warm water
Salt and pepper, to taste

Combine all ingredients in a bowl, adjusting the water if batter is too thick. Allow batter to stand for about 15 minutes.

Preheat a lightly greased griddle or frying pan. Pour a

small amount (about 3" around) into the pan. Wait for bubbles to form and edges to brown before turning. Works as a dinner accompaniment—or omit garlic, onion, and Dijon and serve for breakfast.

Note: There are approximately 15 grams of carbohydrate per pancake.

Basic Cracker And Piecrust Recipe

This recipe is very easy to make. It can be made from any flour to which you are not sensitive, or any ground nut or seed, such as: ground almonds, filberts, cashews, or sunflower seeds; or rice flour, rye flour, millet flour, amaranth flour, garbanzo-bean flour, or a combination of any of the above. (Note that spelt and kamut flours are ancient strains of wheat and may cause problems for wheat-sensitive people.) Batches can be halved, doubled, or tripled successfully—and they freeze well, too.

For a tasty variation, mashed yam, squash, or sweet potato can be added to the mixture—but remember to reduce the water. Chopped dried apricots, raisins, or chopped prunes can be added to a grain-based cracker to make it a cookie.

For the piecrust, I also like to add grated sheep Romano, and chopped fresh basil for a savory mixture. A ground-nut piecrust is more successful when mixed with 3 Tbsp rice flour, or tapioca flour, which helps hold it together. (Nuts can be ground in a food processor.)

Recipe:
1½ cups flour of your choice—either grain, bean, nut, or in
    combination
¾ tsp baking powder or baking soda
¾ tsp salt
⅓ cup oil or butter
⅓ cup cold water

Preheat oven to 350° F.

In a bowl, mix together dry ingredients; add oil. Add water slowly; stir and mix to desired consistency. (Some nut and grain mixtures may require more water.) Let mixture sit for 15 minutes to blend flavors.

Divide dough in half, and place each half on a greased cookie sheet. Roll out dough to ¼" thick. Cut on an angle into diamond shapes, then prick all over with a fork to allow heat to penetrate the mixture. Bake for 10 minutes or until golden brown. Makes 5 dozen crackers.

For a piecrust: Press mixture into greased pie pan, prick with fork, and bake for 10–15 minutes.

Desserts & Beverages

If you want your health to return and your body to rebalance, stay away from sweets. As you may remember from reading *The Body "Knows"* and *The Body "Knows" Diet*, the overconsumption of sugar and carbohydrates is probably our society's number one health challenge.

Everyone needs a little sweet in their lives, but the catch is not to get hooked on even "allowable treats" because of blood sugar fluctuations, Candida yeast overgrowth, and the continuing trap of addiction.

Take a look at the following recipes and assess whether they are worth the effort. Remember, once your body is balanced, you will be able to enjoy an occasional sweet dessert in a restaurant or at a friend's home, without losing major momentum in your health goal. But once your Candida is under control, the great benefit is that you will lose the desire for sweets—truly. And with your newfound energy, you will fill your life with all the things you really want to do.

DESSERTS

Simple and Decadent

5 toasted pecan halves
¼ low-carbohydrate "bar" — purchased from a health-food
   store

Arrange pecan halves on an attractive saucer. Cut the low-carb
bar into 4 equal pieces and store away the remaining 3 pieces for
another occasion—I'm watching! Place your ¼ piece of the bar
on top of the pecans and microwave 10 seconds or until soft.
   Remember "turtles"? This is a benign turtle, and you just
get one—after dinner, with a cup of herbal tea.

Pretend Cookie

When the need for sweets hits, here's a simple idea.
   Take 1 rice cake (10 grams of carbs) or 2 rice crackers (4
grams of carbs) and coat liberally with cashew butter or almond
butter. Sprinkle with stevia, roasted carob, or cinnamon.

Coconut Pecan Crunch*

1 cup clarified butter or coconut oil
2 Tbsp honey or 1 tsp stevia (or to taste)
1 tsp pure vanilla extract
3 Tbsp powdered carob
½–1 cup toasted pecans, walnuts, or a mixture of favorite nuts.
¼ cup unsweetened coconut, shredded (optional)

Butter a 9" square baking pan or 9" pie plate; line the bottom
with roasted nuts and coconut. Melt butter or coconut oil over
very low heat; add honey, vanilla and carob. Pour this mixture

over the nuts. Place directly in freezer, but be sure to stir several times while cooling to prevent butter from rising to the top. In approximately ½ hour when solid, cut and serve. Enjoy one piece after dinner with a cup of herbal tea. (This treat needs to be stored in the freezer.)

Note: This is not suitable for people who have nut or legume allergies. However, there is not enough honey per piece to affect a Candida-eradication program. It is also low in carbohydrates—approximately 8 grams per 1″ square.

*Adapted from Judith Minzel's Carob Treat recipe and used with permission.

Rice Flour Bird's Nest Cookies

1½ cups rice flour
½ cup tapioca starch (available in Asian markets)
¼ tsp baking powder
¼ tsp salt
1 cup butter
2 Tbsp honey; or 1½ tsp stevia or other natural sweetener
½ tsp vanilla
⅓ cup unsweetened coconut, shredded
All-fruit jam
Nut pieces (optional)

Preheat oven to 350° F.
    Cream butter and all dry ingredients until mixed well; add vanilla and honey. Chill mixture in refrigerator for approximately ½ hour. Form into balls, and press one side of the balls into unsweetened coconut. Pat onto greased cookie sheet, with coconut side facing up. Make a small well in the middle of each cookie and drop ¼ tsp all-fruit jam in center. Add a walnut, cashew, or filbert piece into the center if desired. Bake 20

minutes; cool well in refrigerator. Carefully transfer to cookie tin and store in freezer. Makes about 2 dozen large cookies

Take out one at a time (do not thaw) and enjoy after dinner with a cup of herbal tea.

Note: Approximately 20 grams of carbohydrate per cookie. Also, enjoy the Pamela's line of rice flour cookies, which are available at health-food stores.

Rice Pudding

2 cups jasmine (sweet) rice
2 cups water
2 cups coconut milk
2 tsp stevia
1 tsp cinnamon
1 tsp nutmeg

In a medium pan, mix together water, jasmine rice, and 1 cup coconut milk; bring to a boil and reduce to simmer for 15–20 minutes. Add remaining ingredients and stir often to prevent sticking. Rice should be creamy.

Serve with additional coconut milk, sliced mango, berries, and toasted cashews.

Note: This recipe is not low in carbohydrates.

Almond Flour Muffins

This recipe and the one that follows have an almond flour base. (I buy my almond flour from Oh! Nuts: **www.ohnuts.com**. It is also very easy to make: simply grind unroasted almonds in a food processor.) Both recipes are included in this book with grateful thanks to Judith Minzel* and her friend Keri.

½ cup melted butter (or yogurt)
6 eggs
⅛ cup honey
¼ tsp salt
3 cups almond flour
1 tsp baking soda

Preheat oven to 350° F.

Mix together wet ingredients; mix together dry ingredients and add to wet. Grease muffin tin, or insert greased muffin papers into tin. Fill each muffin cup half full and bake for 18–20 minutes. Muffins will brown nicely and are done when a knife inserted comes out clean. This recipe makes 12 muffins.

Variations: Add 2 tsp cinnamon or grated orange or lemon rind, or 1 tsp almond extract. Or leave out the honey and add sheep Romano or goat cheddar cheese; or garlic, onion, or herbs.

Note: There are 6 grams of carbohydrate and 195 calories per muffin.

* Judith Minzel says:

> *I like to get almond flour from Lucy's Kitchen Shop (**www. lucyskitchenshop.com** or 1-888-484-2126). If you get Lucy's cookbook, use ½ to ¼ the amount of honey she uses and things will be plenty sweet! Note that honey is the easiest of all sugars to digest, and in very small quantities is okay. Stevia doesn't work well in baked goods.*
>
> *Keep in mind that although almond flour is low in carbohydrates, it does still have calories, so take it easy! These muffins and scones can be a lifesaver for some people, especially those who are grain sensitive and have trouble gaining weight.*

Keri's Almond Flour Scones

2½ cups almond flour
¾ tsp baking soda
¼ tsp sea salt
¾ tsp cardamom
½ tsp cinnamon
½ cup plain yogurt or goat yogurt
1 Tbsp honey
2 eggs, beaten
¼ cup currants or raisins (dried fruit like sugar *can* affect
    Candida levels)
½ cup walnuts, chopped

Preheat oven to 325° F.

Mix together dry ingredients; mix together wet ingredients and add to dry. Drop large spoonfuls onto greased baking sheet, leaving space between. Bake about 20 minutes, until light brown and solid to the touch. Cool on rack. Makes 10 scones.

Note: There are 16 grams of carbohydrate and 207 calories per scone.

Variations: Leave out the walnuts, currants or raisins, and cardamom. Or try:

1. Apricot & Almond: ¼ cup chopped dried apricots (if very dry, soak in warm water and drain), ½ cup slivered almonds, and ¼ tsp almond extract.

2. Date & Orange: ¼ cup chopped dates, 1 Tbsp grated orange zest, ¼ tsp ground cloves, and ¼ tsp ground nutmeg.

3. Gingerbread: ¼ cup raisins or currants, ½ cup chopped walnuts, ½ tsp ground clove, and ½ tsp ground ginger.

4. You can leave out the honey, fruit, and sweet spices; and instead use your choice of herbs, onion, garlic, or sheep or goat cheese.

Coconut Almond Flour Cookies

This is adapted from the recipe for "Monster Cookies" in Elaine Gottschall's book *Breaking the Vicious Cycle*.

5 cups almond flour
½ cup dried cranberries
1 cup walnut pieces
1 cup fine flake unsweetened coconut
½ cup melted butter
⅓ cup honey*
2 beaten eggs
1 tsp baking soda
⅛ tsp salt

Preheat oven to 325° F.

Mix together all ingredients. Drop by large tablespoonfuls onto a greased baking sheet; press flat with a buttered fork, which prevents sticking. Bake until golden brown (15–20 minutes). Makes 3 dozen cookies.

Variations: In place of cranberries, use raisins or ½ cup chopped dried apricots combined with 1 Tbsp chopped preserved ginger.

* If you are working on Candida yeast control, do not get excessive with honey or dried fruit. But a small amount of honey and a few raisins/cranberries are not going to significantly affect your program. With that in mind, do not eat too many of these cookies at once!

Coconut Cream Treats

We serve these treats at many of our events, and people are amazed at how delicious they are. Coconut cream and coconut oil are healthy fats and help to balance blood sugars.

You'll need about 50–100 tiny foil papers, available in cookware stores—these are the tiny muffin papers traditionally used in candy making.

Melt 2 cups (1 small jar) coconut cream* in a bowl over hot water—stir coconut so that the oil on the top and the pulp on the bottom is mixed together. (The entire jar can be melted in the microwave for 30 seconds once or twice or heated over very low heat in a double boiler, or you can place the jar outside in hot weather.) Pour melted coconut cream into papers, filling ¾ full

Add *any* of the following:

- 1 whole nut, any sort
- ¼ tsp toasted sunflower seeds
- ¼ tsp toasted coconut
- 1–2 chopped pecan halves
- ¼ tsp carob—swirl into melted coconut for a hint of "chocolate," or add a drop of "chocolate stevia" or drop in 2 or 3 carob chips (optional)

Place paper cups on a baking sheet and put in fridge or freezer until hardened. These treats will melt at room temperature, but will keep indefinitely in the refrigerator or freezer. Enjoy 1–3 of them with a cup of herbal tea after dinner.

Variation: Mix equal parts coconut cream or coconut oil and nut butter—almond, cashew, or macadamia. Add 1 tsp vanilla for flavoring. Place mixture in fridge until firm enough to work with; form into balls and roll in fine shredded coconut. Keep in a covered container in fridge. Great for mid-evening snacks. (For additional protein, hemp buds may be added to the coconut cream and nut butter before forming into balls.)

*Coconut cream is available from Tropical Traditions: **www. tropicaltraditions.com.**

Lakanto Lemon Mousse

This dessert recipe comes to me from Donna Gates, well-known author of *The Body Ecology Diet*. My husband and I shared a delightful meal with Donna and her family at her beach house in Jupiter, Florida. This dessert was included, and it was quite rich but so delicious.

3 whole eggs
3 egg yolks
3 egg whites—set aside
½ cup lemon *or* lime juice
1 stick or ½ cup butter
½ cup and 1 Tbsp Lakanto*
2 Tbsp lemon or lime zest (fine grated rind)

Whisk together whole eggs, egg yolks, Lakanto, lemon or lime juice, and zest. Heat in a double boiler over medium heat and whisk constantly until mixture coats a stainless-steel spoon. Let cool for ½ hour, but continue to stir occasionally.

In a glass bowl, beat 3 egg whites until they form stiff peaks; set aside. Gently fold hot mixture into the beaten egg whites—1 spoonful at a time. Do not overmix.

Spoon dessert into parfait glasses and garnish with more zest. Refrigerate 2 hours before serving. Serves 6.

* Lakanto is an alternative sweetener that is widely used in Japan. It has zero calories, is safe for diabetics, and will not alter intestinal flora. You can order Lakanto from Donna's website: **www.bodyecology.com.**

BEVERAGES

When it comes to making healthy changes, the question I am probably asked most is, "How can I replace coffee, or hot or iced black tea?" Quite simply, the very best way you can—and as soon as you can—with something that won't derail your nervous system, agitate your pancreas, increase your heart rate, clog your liver, or cause urinary problems.

There are many delicious herbal-tea combinations out there. For example, sip Celestial Seasonings Vanilla Hazelnut or English Toffee after dinner for a smooth, robust beverage. For daytime, I like white peony, which is low in caffeine; Japanese twig tea, and aromatic jasmine pearl tea—served very weak.

In the winter, you might try a steaming mug of almond milk. Sprinkle with cinnamon or carob powder.

When it comes to healthy choices, think about increasing your water intake. On the weekends I enjoy San Pellegrino, an Italian sparking mineral water served in a goblet with a twist of lemon or lime.

For Children

If you are concerned about your children or grandchildren—and their behavior problems, allergies, runny noses, weight gain, crankiness, or poor energy—you will notice a dramatic difference when you eliminate sugar and dairy products from their diet. This is well worth your effort. (Candida albicans yeast can be a factor in many children as well, because of the overuse of antibiotics.)

Children's symptoms and problems seem to turn around miraculously when offending substances are removed from their diets and environment. It's as simple as that. If you find yourself saying, "I want my child back," I urge you to focus on this area as quickly as possible. Full guidelines for doing a short "clear" test period are in my book *The Body "Knows."*

You will have the best chance for dietary compliance when your children are small— before they are indoctrinated by television and other children. Fortunately, grain allergies in children are not so prevalent, but I urge you to take sugar and dairy products out of the house at once—these are the biggest culprits, along with additives and food dyes.

Substitute honey, maple syrup, and stevia for sweeteners, but use them sparingly. These *are* sweets and they will have an effect on Candida overgrowth, but they will not have a significant effect on mood and behavior.

In place of dairy products, substitute soymilk (if tolerated), rice milk, almond milk, or coconut milk. Some health-food stores even carry potato milk, called "Vegimilk." At any rate, I recommend that these milks only be used for cereal (a healthy variety) or for making "smoothies"—they are not necessary for drinking. Because many alternative milks contain sweeteners such as rice syrup and barley malt, they should only be used in limited amounts. Some children thrive on goat's milk and goat's cheese. There are also other sources of calcium besides any kind of milk or cheese, such as: green, leafy vegetables; nuts; and whole grains. However, calcium supplementation may be necessary.

The best drink there is—and one we need to teach children to get excited about—is WATER. Place a large pitcher of water on the dinner table, and make purified water accessible any time.

Remember, your children are watching you. When you cook, prepare, and serve nutritious meals, they learn what it means to respect the body. As your children grow up, mature, and form their own opinions, they will remember the nutritional foundation that you have given them. They will choose to nourish and respect their own bodies and they will be more likely to choose partners who feel the same way.

This chapter provides my best suggestions for kids, pertaining to each meal of the day.

BREAKFAST

Let's face it—most kids are addicted to cereal. Choose non-sugary cereals from the health-food store, appropriate milks suggested above, a handful of roasted nuts sprinkled on top with a few berries. For sweetener, use powdered stevia.

Give your child adequate protein at breakfast: eggs (note

that eggs are a common allergen, especially for young children), turkey sausage, turkey meatballs (see my recipe on page 47), turkey bacon, soy bacon, etc. For toast, use alternative bread.

LUNCH

Hot lunches at school are a real problem. Macaroni and cheese (there's that dairy again), the forced "milk program," Jell-O, and all the rest of it—how are kids supposed to learn and behave on this junk?

If you have a highly allergic child or one with behavior problems, carrying a sack lunch may be the only answer. Include: a sandwich with protein filling, or almond butter and a very light spread of all-fruit jelly; a small package of roasted, unsalted nuts; fruit for dessert; bottled water or pure juice to drink; cut-up vegetables; cut-up chunks of cold meat; goat-cheese chunks; and/or a small bag of healthy chips.

DINNER

Most children will enjoy any of the recipes in this book except perhaps the more sophisticated ones. Slow-cooker meals in particular work very well for busy families. If you prepare a pot of steamed rice, a meal is created—with leftovers!

Teach your child to help you in the kitchen. A six-year-old can make a salad, and a much younger child can set the table.

When a baby is weaned and starts solid food, smart parents hand blend a small portion of the food that they are having and feed it to the baby. Always check with your doctor regarding the right time to introduce your baby to certain foods.

Sneaky Cauliflower Chicken Noodle Bake

This is a favorite of my niece Georgia and her son, Kylan.

8 oz. brown rice pasta (penne, rotini, or macaroni)
1 Tbsp olive oil
1 lb boneless skinless chicken breasts
1 tsp Italian seasoning
One (28 oz) jar organic spaghetti sauce
2 cups fresh cauliflower, chopped *really* fine
2 cups goat mozzarella cheese, shredded
¼ cup rice milk

Preheat oven to 350° F.

Grease a 9" x 13" baking dish with olive oil. Cook pasta according to package directions for "al dente"; drain. Pour into prepared baking dish.

Heat oil in a large saucepan or Dutch oven over medium-high heat. While oil is heating, cut chicken breasts into bite-size pieces; brown chicken in oil. Add Italian seasoning and spaghetti sauce; let simmer 2–3 minutes. Add to chicken and tomato-sauce mixture; simmer. Stir in cauliflower; cook another minute until it wilts slightly. Pour chicken mixture over pasta. Top with 1 cup of the shredded mozzarella. Bake, uncovered, for 20 minutes or until bubbly

Note: You can add garden peas, baby carrots, sweet corn, or other child-friendly veggies to this. The cauliflower adds nutrients to the dish, and kids don't even know it's there!

DESSERTS

No dessert is necessary after a hearty dinner—save it for special occasions. I frequently see clients who struggle with weight gain and health issues because they grew up with desserts every day. Do your best not to set that pattern with your own children.

See the Desserts chapter in this cookbook for ideas. Keep in mind that cut-up fruit is also a great choice—or try the three suggestions below.

Smoothie:
1 cup fresh fruit
1 cup alternative milk
4 ice cubes

Blend at high speed for 2 minutes.

Frozen Banana:
When bananas are overripe, freeze them in a large Ziploc bag. When needed, take 1 out, cut into chunks, and blend at high speed. Sprinkle a little cinnamon or roasted carob and chopped toasted almonds on top, and serve.

Pretend Cookie:
1 rice cake or 2-4 rice crackers spread with nut butter and sprinkled with stevia, roasted carob, or cinnamon.

SNACKS

I suggest that you create a "snack cupboard" that is accessible for your kids, and each child can pick 1 snack item at the appropriate time from this cupboard. Load it up with wholesome "chips," healthy crackers, non-sugary fruit leather, pure juices, or toasted nuts.

Nut butters in place of peanut butter on whole-grain crackers also make a great snack. Soy cheese, cut-up vegetables, chunks of protein, and roasted nuts set out on a tray make an appealing snack for the whole family. For picky eaters, a snack tray like this ensures that they're getting appropriate nutrition without the usual dinnertime trials.

––––––––––––––––––––

It has been my pleasure to introduce you to a whole new world of eating. I wish you and your family the very best of health and happiness.

— *Caroline*

––––––––––––––––––––

Carbohydrate Gram Counter

Food	Amount	Carbohydrate Grams
ANIMAL PROTEIN		
Chicken, Beef, Fish,		0
Lamb, Turkey, Veal, Pork,		
(Ham, Bacon)		
Shellfish, Wild meats, Eggs		
DAIRY PRODUCTS		
Whole milk	1 cup	12
Ice cream	½ cups	15
Cheese	1 oz hard	1
Cottage cheese	½ cup	4
Sour cream	1 Tbsp	1
Yogurt	½ cup	8
FATS		
Butter	1 Tbsp	0
French dressing	1 Tbsp	2
Vegetable oil	unlimited	0
Olive oil	unlimited	0
Mayonnaise	1 Tbsp	0
NUTS		
Mixed	¼ cup	5
Almonds	¼ cup	5
Peanut butter	2 Tbsp	5
Cashew nut butter	2 Tbsp	11

FOOD	AMOUNT	CARBOHYDRATE GRAMS

VEGETABLES

Food	Amount	Carbohydrate Grams
Alfalfa sprouts (raw)	½ cup	
Arugula	unlimited	0
Artichoke	1 medium	14
Asparagus	10 spears	4
Beans, green.	1 cup, cooked	8
Beets	1 cup, cooked	6
Broccoli	1 cup, cooked	5
Brussels sprouts	6	5
Cabbage	1 cup, raw & shredded	3
Cabbage	1 cup, cooked	5
Carrots	1 medium, raw	5
Carrots	1 cup, cooked	12
Cauliflower	1 cup	4
Celery	2 stalks	2
Corn	1 ear	20
Cucumber	1 medium	6
Eggplant	1 cup, cooked	6
Kale	1 cup, cooked	3
Lettuce	unlimited	0
Okra	1 cup	11
Onions	½ cup, raw	5
Onions	½ cup, cooked	10
Green peas	1 cup	20
Green pepper	1 large	5
Potatoes	1 small	20
Spinach	1 cup, cooked	4
Squash	1 cup, cooked	10
Tomatoes	1 medium	4
Turnip	½ cup	8
Ketchup	1 Tbsp	5
Tomato juice	1 cup	5

FOOD	AMOUNT	CARBOHYDRATE GRAMS

BEANS (LEGUMES)

Food	Amount	Carbohydrate Grams
Tofu	½ cup	20
Lima beans	½ cup	25
Kidney beans	½ cup	13
White beans	½ cup	22
Fava beans	½ cup	16
Soy flour	½ cup	12

FRUIT

Food	Amount	Carbohydrate Grams
Apples	1 large	20
Apricots	4	14
Avocado	½	5
Banana	1 medium	25
Strawberries	1 cup	7
Raspberries	1 cup	8
Blackberries	1 cup	10
Blueberries	1 cup	17
Cantaloupe	1 cup	12
Grapefruit	½ small	8
Grapes	½ cup	8
Lemons	1 medium	8
Lime	1 medium	8
Orange	1 small	11
Orange juice	1 cup	22
Peach	1 medium	8
Pear	1 medium	20
Pineapple	1 cup	17
Pineapple	½ cup, canned	18
Plum	1 large	18
Watermelon	1 cup	11

Food	Amount	Carbohydrate Grams
BREADS & CEREALS		
Bagel	1	27
Bread	1 slice	20
Hamburger bun	1	23
English muffin	1	25
Pita round	1	20
Rice cake	1	8
Rice crackers	2	4
Saltine cracker	1	2
Wasa (rye) cracker	1	7
Cornflakes	1 cup	17
Oatmeal	1 cup, cooked	20
Shredded wheat	1 large	23
Spaghetti, macaroni, pasta	1 cup	25
Noodles (egg)	1 cup	26
Rice	1 cup, cooked	20
SWEETENERS		
Honey	1 Tbsp	15
White sugar	1 tsp	4
Brown sugar	1 Tbsp	10
Stevia (herb sweetener)	1 tsp	1
Syrup	1 Tbsp	15
SPIRITS		
Wine (red or white)	1 glass	3
Light Beer	8 oz	4

For a complete list of carbohydrate grams refer to *Protein Power,* by Michael and Mary Dan Eades

FOOD FAMILIES

The following is a list of common food families. When avoiding *offending* foods, it can be helpful to check the food family list and avoid foods that are in the same family.

* Single food families.

PLANTS

APPLE
Apple
Apple Cider
Pear
Pectin
Quince & Seed
Vinegar

BAMBOO
SHOOTS*

BANANA
Arrowroot
Banana
Plantain

BARLEY
Malt

BEET
Beet
Beet Sugar
Chard
Lamb Quarters
Spinach
Thistle

BIRCH
Filbert
Hazelnut
Wintergreen

BRAZIL NUT*
Brazil Nut

BUCKWHEAT
Buckwheat
Garden sorrel

Rhubarb

CACTUS
Cactus
Prickly Pear
Tequila

CANE
Sugar
Molasses

CAPER*
Capers

CARROT
Carrots
Celeriac
Celery
Coriander

Cumin
Dill
Fennel
Parsley
Parsnip

CASHEW
Cashew
Mango
Pistachio

CHICORY*

CITRUS
Angostura
Citron
Grapefruit
Kumquat
Lemon
Lime
Orange
Tangerine

COCOA BEAN
Cocoa
Cocoa chocolate
Cola bean

COMPOSITE
Artichoke
Dandelion
Endive
Escarole
Jerusalem
   artichoke
Lettuce

Sesame oil Sesame
   seed
Sunflower oil
Sunflower seed

CORN
Dextrose (Glucose)
Meal
Oil
Starch
Sugar
Syrup

EBONY
Persimmon

FUNGI
Baker's yeast
Brewer's yeast
Mold
Mushroom

GINGER
Cardamom
Ginger
Turmeric

GOOSE-BERRY
Currant
Gooseberry

GOURD
Casaba
Cantaloupe
Cucumber
Gherkin

Honeydew
Muskmelon
Persian melon
Pumpkin
Squash
Watermelon

GRAPE
Brandy
Champagne
Cream of tartar
Grapes
Raisin
Wine
Wine vinegar

HEATH
Blueberry
Cranberry
Huckleberry

IRIS
Saffron

LAUREL
Avocado
Bay leaves
Cinnamon
Sassafras

LILY
Aloes
Asparagus
Chives
Garlic
Leek

Onion
Sarsaparilla

LEGUMES
Black-eyed pea
Carob
Green pea
Jack bean
Kidney bean
Lecithin
Lentil
Licorice
Lima bean
Navy bean
Peanut and oil
Pinto
Senna
Soybean
Soy oil
Soy flour
String bean
Tonka bean

MADDER*
Coffee

MALLOW
Cottonseed meal
Cottonseed oil
Okra (Gumbo)

MAPLE
Maple sugar
Maple syrup

MILLET*

MINT
Basil
Horehound
Marjoram
Mint
Oregano
Peppermint
Sage
Spearmint
Thyme

MORNING
  GLORY
Sweet potato
Yam

MULBERRY
Breadfruit
Fig
Hop
Mulberry

MUSTARD
Broccoli
Cabbage
Cauliflower
Chinese cabbage
Collard
Horseradish
Kale
Kohlrabi
Kraut
Mustard
Mustard greens

Mustard seeds
Radish
Rape (canola)
Rutabaga
Sprouts
Swedes
Turnips
Watercress

MYRTLE
Allspice
Cloves
Guava
Paprika
Pimento

NIGHTSHADE
Belladonna
Black pepper
Chili pepper
Green pepper
Eggplant
Potato
Red cayenne
Red capsicum
Red pepper
Tobacco
Tomato
White pepper

NUTMEG
Mace
Nutmeg

OAK
Chestnut

OATS*

OLIVE
Black olives
Green olives
Olive oil

ORCHID
Vanilla

PALM
Coconut
Date
Palm cabbage
Sago

PARSLEY
Anise
Angelica
Caraway
Celery
Celery seed
Carrots
Celeriac
Coriander
Cumin
Dill
Fennel
Parsley
Parsnips

PAWPAW
Pawpaw

Papain
Papaya

PINE
Juniper
Pinion Nut

PINEAPPLE

POMEGRANATE

POPPY*
Poppy seeds

PLUM
Almond
Apricot
Cherry
Nectarine
Peach
Plum
Prune
Wild cherry

RICE*

RYE*

ROSE
Blackberry
Boysenberry
Dewberry
Loganberry

Raspberry
Strawberry
Youngberry

SOAPBERRY
Lichi Nut

TAPIOCA*

TEA*

WALNUT
Black walnut
English walnut
Hickory nut
Pecan

WHEAT
Bran
Farina
Flour
Gluten Flour
Wheat germ
Whole wheat

WILD RICE*

MEAT

-Butter
-Cheese
-Gelatin

BIRDS
Chicken
Chicken eggs
Duck
Duck eggs
Goose
Goose eggs
Guinea hen
Grouse
Partridge
Pheasant
Squab
Turkey
Turkey eggs

FISH*

CRUSTACEANS
Crab
Crayfish
Lobster
Shrimp

MAMMALS
Beef
 -butter
 -cheese
 -gelatin
 -milk
 -veal
Buffalo
Goat
 -Milk
 -Cheese
 -Mutton

Lamb
Pork
 -Bacon
 -Ham
Rabbit
Venison

MOLLUSKS
Abalone
Clam
Mussel
Oyster
Scallop
Snail
Squid

Hidden Food Sources

You may be surprised to find that your favorite foods are hiding out in the most unlikely places. This list can help you to identify *offending* foods, which could be hidden in other products. Read labels and get to know the ingredients of common, combination foods.

EGG
Baking powders
Bavarian cream
Breaded foods
Breads
Cake flours
Cakes
Custards
Eggs
French toast
Fritters
Frostings
Frying batters
Griddle cakes
Hamburger
  patties
Hollandaise sauce
Ice cream
Icings
Macaroni

Macaroons
Marshmallows
Mayonnaise
Meat loaf
Meringues
Noodles
Pancakes
Puddings
Rolls
Salad dressings
Sauces
Sausages
Soufflés
Waffles

YEAST
Beer
Bovril
Brandy
Breads

Buns
Cakes
Cereals
Cheeses
Chocolate
Condiments
Cookies
Crackers
French dressing
Fruit juices
Gin
Horseradish
Malted milk
Mayonnaise
Olives
Pastries
Pickles
Pretzels
Rolls
Rum

Sauerkraut
Soy sauce
Tomato sauce
Truffles
Vinegar
Vitamins
Vodka
Whiskey
Wine

WHEAT
Bagels
Biscuits
Bologna
Bread
Breaded meats/
   fish
Cakes
Cereals
Cookies
Corn bread
Crackers
Doughnuts
Dumplings
Flour
Gravies
Hot cakes
Liverwurst
Lunch meats
Macaroni
Pasta
Pie crust

SOYBEANS
Baby foods
Biscuits

Breads
Butter substitute
Cakes
Cereals
Cooking spray
Crackers
Hard candies
Ice cream
Lecithin
Lunch meats
Margarine
Mayonnaise
Milk substitute
Oils
Oriental sauces
Pastries
Salad dressings
Soups
Soy flour
Soy noodles
Tempura
Textured vegetable
   protein
Tofu

MILK
Biscuits
Breads
Buttermilk
Cakes
Cheese
Cheese dishes
Chocolate milk
Chowders
Cookies
Creamed foods

Custards
Fritters
Gravies
Ice cream
Malted cocoa
Mashed potatoes
Omelets
Ovaltine
Pancakes
Pancake mix
Potatoes,
   scalloped
Powdered milk
Salad dressing,
   creamy
Sherbets
Soda crackers
Soufflés
Soups, creamed
Sour cream
Waffles
Whey
Yogurt

CORN
All baked goods
Aspirin
Baking powder
Beer, ales
Biscuits
Breads, pastries
Butter substitute
Cakes, cookies
Candies
Carbonated
   beverages

Catsup	Gravies	Puddings, instant
Chewing gum	Grits	Salad dressing
Cornmeal	Gummed papers	Sandwich spreads
Corn oil	Instant teas	Sausages
Cough syrups	Margarine	Soups, creamed
Cream pies	Non-dairy	Stamp glue
Cured hams	creamers	Starch
Custard	Pancake mix	Toothpaste
Doughnuts	Pie Crusts	Tortillas
Graham crackers	Popcorn	Whiskey

USEFUL BOOKS

Breaking the Vicious Cycle: Intestinal Health Through Diet, by
   Elaine Gottshall (Kirkton Press)
From Belly Fat to Belly Flat, by C.W. Randolph, M.D.; and
   Genie James (Health Communications, Inc.)
*Nourishing Traditions: The Cookbook that Challenges Politically
   Correct Nutrition and the Diet Dictocrats,* by Sally Fallon,
   with Mary G. Enig, Ph.D. (New Trends Publishing)
Protein Power, by Michael R. Eades, M.D.; and Mary Dan
   Eades, M.D. (Bantam)
*Sugar Shock!: How Sweets and Simple Carbs Can Derail Your
   Life—and How You Can Get Back on Track,* by Connie
   Bennett, C.H.H.C., with Stephen T. Sinatra, M.D. (Berkley
   Trade)
*The Body Ecology Diet: Recovering Your Health and Rebuilding
   Your Immunity,* by Donna Gates and Linda Schatz (Body
   Ecology)
*The Belly Fat Cure: Discover the New Carb Swap System and Lose
   4 to 9 lbs. Every Week,* by Jorge Cruise (Hay House, Inc.)
The Gluten-Free Almond Flour Cookbook, by Elana Amsterdam
   (Celestial Arts)
The Rosedale Diet: Turn Off Your Hunger Switch!, by Ron
   Rosedale, M.D.; and Carol Colman (HarperCollins)
The Yeast Connection: A Medical Breakthrough, by William G.
   Crook, M.D. (Vintage)
Virgin Coconut Oil, by Brian and Marianita Jader Shilhavy
   (Tropical Traditions, Inc.)

We Band of Mothers: Autism, My Son, and the Specific Carbohydrate Diet, by Judith Chinitz, with Sidney M. Baker, M.D. (Autism Research Institute)

For other useful gluten-free, dairy-free cookbooks, check out: **www.scdkitchen.com/cookbook.html**.

A note about cookbooks: Even though a cookbook may be allergen free, it does not mean that all of the recipes are suitable for you. Watch for specific food allergens, high-carb recipes, and hidden sweets. Honey, agave nectar, maple syrup, rice syrup, barley malt, and other sugars *all* need to be kept to a minimum.

Caroline Sutherland's Products

Books

The Body "Knows": How to Tune In to Your Body and Improve Your Health
A primer for understanding health and developing intuition. $14.95

The Body "Knows" Diet: Cracking the Weight-Loss Code
Identifies the five components of successful weight loss. $16.95

The Body Knows . . . How to Stay Young
Help for healthy aging. $15.95

Mommy, I Hurt . . . Mommy, I Love You
A self-help guide for parents and children. This little book inspires parents to help their children over the "rough spots" in a unique, reassuring way, using the principles of relaxation therapy and creative visualization. $10.00

DVDs

The Body "Knows"
Excerpts from Caroline's speeches and classes. $19.95

The Heart of the Family
This parent education DVD covers a variety of topics showing unique ways to strengthen communication between parent and child and blended family members. (2 hours) $22.00

CDs

The Body "Knows" about Hormones, 4-CD Set
Four hours of interviews with Caroline and Larry Frieders, R.Ph., regarding the latest information about bioidentical hormone balancing. $39.95

Tibetan Power Meditation
This deep, powerful meditation CD aligns you to the awesome majesty of Mount Everest, the vast Tibetan skies, and the sacred peace of Emerald Lake. Adults (60 minutes) $19.95

Letting Go of the Past & Moving Forward
Have you ever felt unable to let go of the past? Release old resentments and grievances with soothing reassurance repeated nightly. Caroline's restful, encouraging voice gives you the confidence to move forward and the willingness to let go. Soothing wave background. Adults (60 minutes) $19.95

Fountain of Youth – for Women
Deep relaxation and positive programming for women in all phases of menopause. This CD really helps with personal motivation, anxiety, and sleeplessness. Soothing wave background. Adults (60 minutes) $19.95

Fountain of Youth – for Men
Deep relaxation and positive programming for the vibrantly aging male. This CD helps with motivation, inner strength, and personal empowerment while promoting deep sleep. Soothing wave background. Adults (60 minutes) $19.95

Couples – Serenity & Tranquility
This CD works to remove blocks to a loving, healthy relationship. In a few short weeks, experience a deeper level of joy

and bonding with your loved one and with yourself. Soothing wave background. Adults (60 minutes) $19.95

Body Alive — Deep Relaxation & Sleep
You're guided through a series of phrases about health, immunity, weight control, and abundant energy, as well as improving sleep—great for insomniacs. Soothing, positive wave sounds. Adults (60 minutes) $19.95

Overcoming Jet Lag, Travel Fatigue, or Fear of Flying
A very effective CD, recommended by travelers, flight attendants, pilots, and businesspeople for jet lag and fear of flying. Soothing wave background. Adults (60 minutes) $19.95

Meditation & Music
A relaxing guided-meditation CD designed to center you, focus the breath, work with your own affirmations, and help to access that deep state of peace within you. This CD is set to beautiful music, created by award-winning musician Paul Armitage. Adults (60 minutes) $19.95

Motivation & Confidence for Teenagers & Young People
Parents say this CD can put the *terrific* back into your teenager. In three to four weeks of nightly listening, teenagers can expect to feel an increase in self-esteem, motivation, and positive choices. Soothing wave background. Adolescents ages 12 and over (60 minutes) $19.95

Ace Those Exams!
Decreases the fear and anxiety of exams, while increasing memory and mental ability. Really works for teens *and* adults! Soothing wave background. Adults and adolescents, ages 12 & over (60 minutes) $19.95

Children's Products

My Little Angel Gift Sets
Welcome to the world of Angels 4 Kids®—angels, CDs, and storybooks that reassure and encourage children. All sets include a soft, cuddly angel, which is handmade and machine washable in soft cotton velour, and a positive, uplifting 60-minute story/music CD. Angels come with white or ethnic (brown) faces and are suitable for both boys and girls, ages toddler to teenager.

— *My Little Angel Tells Me I'm Special®*. This story helps children fall asleep and build self-esteem. A general CD that's useful for all children—babies to 10 years (adults and teens love them, too). Cost per angel set: $24.95

— *My Little Angel Helps Me and My Family®*. This story supports and comforts children who are adjusting to a family breakup, separation, or divorce. Cost per angel set: $24.95

— *My Little Angel Helps Me in the Hospital®*. This story calms, comforts, and reassures children who require hospitalization for major or minor surgery, serious illness, cancer treatment, burns, or any surgical procedure. Cost per angel set: $24.95

— *My Little Angel Loves Me®* This story reassures, comforts, and supports children (and adults) who have been abused, traumatized, or mistreated. Cost per angel set: $24.95

Body Alive (Children) — Confidence & Self-Esteem CD
Helps your child to understand body processes, as well as developing a healthy attitude about food choices, physical activity, confidence, and positive values. Set to beautiful music. Ages 3–10 (60 minutes) $19.95

School Work & Making Friends CD
Helps to develop love and excitement about school and learning as well as helping the child to overcome blocks and barriers to playing and sharing with others. Set to enchanting music. Ages 3–10 (60 minutes) $19.95

The Changing Family – Feeling Safe and Secure CD
Helps to reassure and comfort children in a changing family situation such as a divorce or separation. Ages 3–10 (60 minutes) $19.95

To find out more about Caroline Sutherland and her books, products, seminars, and teleconferences, visit:
www.carolinesutherland.com.

About the Author

Caroline Sutherland has a vast clinical background as an allergy-testing technician in environmental medicine, where her intuitive gift developed. She was raised in a medical family in which both her father and grandfather were medical doctors. As a child, the "blueprint" of her family lineage created important seeds for her future career as a medical intuitive. For more than 25 years, she has lectured internationally on the subject, and her intuitive impressions have positively impacted the lives of more than 100,000 people.

Caroline is the author of numerous books and audio programs on health, personal development, and self-esteem; as well as the founder of Sutherland Communications, which offers medical-intuitive training, weight-loss programs, and consultation services for adults and children. She is a popular guest on radio and television.

CPSIA information can be obtained at www.ICGtesting.com
Printed in the USA
LVOW122029201011

251426LV00001B/9/P